A Few Good Memories

Tales from

Marine Corps Boot Camp

Bob Taylor

TRAFFORD

© 2001 by Robert A. Taylor. All rights reserved.

No part of this publication may be reproduced, stored in a retrieval system, or transmitted, in any form or by any means, electronic, mechanical, photocopying, recording, or otherwise, without the written prior permission of the author.

Author invites email comments: roarta@hotmail.com

National Library of Canada Cataloguing in Publication Data

Taylor, Bob, 1933-
   A few good memories : tales from USMC boot camp

ISBN 1-55369-144-X

   1. United States. Marine Corps—Military life. 2. United States. Marine Corps—Anecdotes. I. Title.

V736.T39 2002   359.9'6'0973   C2001-904269-8

TRAFFORD

This book was published *on-demand* in cooperation with Trafford Publishing.
On-demand publishing is a unique process and service of making a book available for retail sale to the public taking advantage of on-demand manufacturing and Internet marketing.
On-demand publishing includes promotions, retail sales, manufacturing, order fulfilment, accounting and collecting royalties on behalf of the author.

Suite 6E, 2333 Government St., Victoria, B.C. V8T 4P4, CANADA
Phone   250-383-6864   Toll-free   1-888-232-4444 (Canada & US)
Fax   250-383-6804   E-mail   sales@trafford.com
Web site   www.trafford.com   TRAFFORD PUBLISHING IS A DIVISION OF TRAFFORD HOLDINGS LTD.
Trafford Catalogue #01-0546   www.trafford.com/robots/01-0546.html

10   9   8   7   6   5   4   3   2

ACKNOWLEDGEMENTS

Without the assistance of hundreds of Marines who sent in stories,

and of the Marines at Parris Island,

including

Brigadier General Cheney,

Staff Sergeant Fetzer,

and

Master Sergeant Shearer,

I could never have completed this book.

Dedication

This book is dedicated to my wife, Marjorie. She had faith that I could complete a task such as this. At times I thought she was wrong.

Contents

Chapter 1.....Pg 1..... Digging for Gold
Chapter 2.....Pg 5......Zeroing In
Chapter 3.....Pg 10.....Acquiring
Chapter 4.....Pg 14.....Waiting
Chapter 5.....Pg 19.....The Beginning
Chapter 6.....Pg 26.....Receiving
Chapter 7.....Pg 35.....Getting Started
Chapter 8.....Pg 45.....The Corps Means Business
Chapter 9.....Pg 51.....Adjustments to Military Life
Chapter 10...Pg 56.....Mail Call
Chapter 11...Pg 62.....Physical Conditioning
Chapter 12...Pg 70.....Cleanliness
Chapter 13...Pg 74.....Gotchas
Chapter 14...Pg 79.....Mess Duty
Chapter 15...Pg 83.....Close Order Drill
Chapter 16...Pg 87.....Combat Pool
Chapter 17...Pg 92.....Movement Under Fire
Chapter 18...Pg 97.....Gung-Ho Events
Chapter 19...Pg 106.....The Crucible
Chapter 20...Pg 111.....Graduation
Chapter 21...Pg 114.....Home
Appendix 1...Pg 117....The Drill Instructor
Appendix 2...Pg 130....Letters from Bryan
Appendix 3...Pg 147....A New Look at Creationism
Appendix 4...Pg 150....A Few Boot Camp Statistics
Appendix 5...Pg 152....The Recruit

A Few Good Memories

1: Digging For Gold

Marine recruits don't just show up at the gates of Parris Island or San Diego for boot camp. Someone must search out qualified young men and women and lead them to sign on the dotted line. Allen G., a retired Marine, remembers the day his interesting life as a Communications Unit Chief at Camp Lejeune, North Carolina, took an abrupt change. He received orders to Recruiting School. After a few weeks of training, he spent the next three years beating the bushes, roaming the streets, and convincing good men and women to apply to become Marines.

Allen lives in Texas now. He fishes a lot now, but remembers that three-year hitch as a Marine recruiter. The story he tells illustrates one of the humorous situations that many recruiters encounter:

In 1967, the Marines needed lots of good men. Vietnam was in full swing and recruiters were pushed to the limit to fill expanded quotas. This young fellow barely 18 years old, whom I remember as James, came in one day. He said he had a goofy job and wanted something exciting to do.

A Few Good Memories

We sat down and looked at opportunities in the Marine Corps. He seemed to be interested, so I gave him some literature and told him I'd call him in a few days. Two days later I called and arranged to meet him at his home with his parents that evening.

I got there and we all went into the dining room. I laid all my stuff out on the table. James and his dad were interested. His mom seemed worried and asked a million questions; but everything seemed to be going like they told us in recruiter school.

Then the crowning question popped from James' mom. "Is there any way that James can sign up and go down to Parris Island for a week or so? Then if it's not like he thought it would be, could his commanding officer let him pack up and come back home?"

I finally signed James a few months later. He came in and told me he had been to see the Air Force, the Army, Navy, and the Coast Guard recruiters. "The more I think about it," he said, "probably nobody else is as good as the Marines. Sign me up."

I did, but without the guarantee that his mama had wanted.

Allen was an interesting man—a real Marine. He said that during his three years of recruiting, he made a lot of mistakes in spite of his excellent training. At first he set his sights too high. He would look for what he calls "Type A+" people: those who fear little and consider themselves to be the greatest, the absolute supreme. It took a lot of turning of rocks, but when he found one, he or she turned out to be loaded with egotism or arrogance, and would never have cut it in the Corps.

Allen finally realized that real Marines are manufactured from kids; good solid kids. They come from the farms, the cities. They're just plain good Americans. They don't consider themselves to be God's gift to the Corps. They do, however, have a solid desire *to become the best.*

A Few Good Memories

Were it not for thousands of Marine Corps recruiters who comb the countryside, talking to kids and their parents, distributing literature, and explaining the advantages of joining the Corps, we could shut down the recruit depots at Parris Island and San Diego. Our entire national defense system could be at risk. Our shores could suddenly be open to any aggressor with a notion to confiscate or destroy this great land of ours.

More and more, when it comes to serving in the military, many Americans would rather let someone else do it; or worse, not have it done at all. Bumper stickers shout distressing messages, such as the one that appeared recently on the bumper of a middle-school teacher's automobile. It read, "It'll be a great day when schools get all the money they need, and the Air Force has to hold a bake sale to buy a new bomber."

Would more and more money produce better results? Probably not. Simply throwing money at a problem is not a solution to fixing it. And as far as holding a bake sale for a new bomber, let us bow our heads in thanks that this mentality was not present in 1941. Had it been, we might be living now under the Nazi Swastika or the Japanese Rising Sun.

What is the secret ingredient that causes a transformation of recruits to Marines? Is it merely raising the right hand in front of some sharp-looking NCO recruiter? Is it watching those old John Wayne movies? Maybe it's seeing those magnificent looking humans pictured in the Marine Corps recruiting posters in front of post office buildings?

Or, is it possible that some kind of rare essence has floated around in our air since November 10, 1775, the date our Corps sprang to life? Maybe only enough of the essence exists for a just a few good men and women. And maybe when its energy is absorbed, it instills a burning desire to become part of the finest fighting organization on earth and gives Marines the savage and ferocious ability on the field of battle. Maybe this is why we, as Marines, wear the eagle, globe, and anchor so proudly.

During this writer's years in the Corps, a lot of Marines crossed my path. I have come to a conclusion that no strange essence is circling the earth. Being a Marine is not by chance. I believe the real answer is programmed deeply within certain people at birth. Only those individuals born with a deep-rooted desire to be the unconditional best would dare pick up the pen and sign on the dotted line. No one is forced to become a Marine. (Can you imagine Chesty Puller in Air Force blue or Army tan?) The Corps is a matter of personal choice. Thanks to God that our country still births brave young souls. And for the good of our country, let us pray that it will continue.

2: Zeroing In

Recruiting is tough, especially in times with no compulsory military obligation. Marine Recruiter Staff Sergeant Mike Gross is one of the 2000 Marines, sailors, and civilians responsible for recruiting in the Eastern Recruiting Region. His home station is Tallahassee, Florida, but he usually works out of his sub-office in Thomasville, Georgia. Thomasville, which is 30 miles north of Tallahassee, is one of 23 recruiting stations in the Eastern Region.

Mike says that most kids are eager to talk. Kids like to be seen talking to Marine recruiters. It gives them a certain status. The hard part is sorting out that serious-minded prospect.

Like most of Mike's fellow recruiters, he spends his days searching for young men and women of the Thomasville area to answer their country's call. He's in his office early, doing paperwork so that he can hit the street about 0800. Mike's monthly quota is to send three qualified recruits through the gate of Parris Island. Rarely does he fail to meet that quota.

Mike's Marine Corps MOS (Military Occupational Specialty) is motor transport, but like a lot of good Marines, he's serving a voluntary three-year tour of duty as a recruiter. He'll be returning to his usual duties in the summer of 2002, but while he's recruiting, he wants to be sure that any recruit that he signs is one who will do a good job. Who knows? Maybe one day they'll work for him in the same unit. If so, he wants Marines who'll produce results.

To recruit-prospects who appear acceptable, Mike gives as much information as possible. He'll provide them with brochures and booklets describing opportunities in the Corps. After a first look at all the colorful, action-packed pamphlets, some prospects are ready for a second look.

Recruiting is expensive and time-consuming. Many of Mike's signups are young people who, at first, reject the idea of military service. A first-contact also helps Mike make a decision as to which prospects he will accept. The Marine Corps is looking for *a Few Good Men and Women*. Not everyone qualifies. The Corps wants good people, not problems.

Jimmy B. was another hard-working headhunter. He served as a Marine recruiter in Metairie, Louisiana, from 1976 through 1979. Vietnam was history and the Corps was releasing lots of battle-weary veterans. New blood was needed to train and replace these old hands for the peacetime Marine Corps. Here is his story about how some kids tend to use recruiters for personal gain:

> *From 1976 through 1979, I spent a lot of time in the high schools of Metairie, Louisiana, talking to recruit-prospects and trying to get kids to join the Corps. The job was tough at that time because of the negative press about Vietnam, which had just ended. The flower child and hippie mentality had trickled down to the high schools.*
>
> *I usually seated myself in a corner of the school libraries. There it was quiet. Besides, most kids eventually came through the library. Some of the kids were adventurous and liked to talk to me. I remember this one lad, a senior named Roger. He would come over and sit at my table almost every time I was there.*
>
> *Invariably, this attractive, blonde-haired, cheerleader-type girl named Lucy would come in when*

A Few Good Memories

Roger and I were talking. Sometimes she would sit at our table for a few minutes and listen to parts of our conversation. When she was there, Roger would ask gung-ho questions about ferocious subjects such as bayonet fighting, the rifle range, and whether I thought he could qualify to go to jump school and become a Pathfinder. It was obvious that Roger and the girl were in a boyfriend-girlfriend relationship and that he was her hero. It was also obvious that Roger wanted to astound his girl friend as much as she wanted to be impressed.

One day I realized that Roger had not been to see me for quite a while. I wondered why. I searched him out and found him in the gym. "Roger, where have you been?" I asked. Roger told me that he and Lucy had broken up and that he had been talking to me mostly because he wanted her to think that he was going to be a Marine.

I invited him to come back and talk seriously about the Corps. Roger never did. It was another of those obvious but sometimes hard-to-recognize and time-wasting situations that they taught us about in recruiter school. I learned from this. I had been had!

Sam O. was a Marine recruiter in 1960. Sam served his recruiting tour in Athens, Georgia. Not only did he have loads of prospects in the high schools, but also the administration offices of the University of Georgia were right around the corner from his office—in full view of the students. Sam discovered that people join the services for various reasons. Listen to his story of how he recruited three young men:

The University of Georgia had celebrated homecoming during a chilly fall weekend in Athens. Homecoming at Georgia was always rowdy and riotous, and the previous weekend was no exception. Someone had told me that a large explosion had occurred in Fraternity Row, but apparently there were no injuries. I had no idea that I was about to become part of it.

A Few Good Memories

About 11:00 a.m., three University of Georgia students came into my office, accompanied by the Athens chief of police. Rick seemed to be the leader and acted as spokesman. He told me that two days prior to homecoming, the three of them had driven up to Chattanooga, Tennessee, and borrowed a cannon from Lookout Mountain State Park. The park marked the site of a vicious battle during the Civil war. Rebel forces had used the cannon in the Battle of Lookout Mountain almost a hundred years before.

The three students brought the cannon back to Athens and set it up on the second-story landing of their fraternity house. On Saturday night after the football game, parties began with enthusiasm on Fraternity Row. At the stroke of midnight, the three boys poked a fused stick of dynamite into the breech of the cannon. Then they inserted a bottle of vodka down into the barrel as a projectile. They pointed the cannon at the fraternity house next door, lit the fuse, and ran for cover.

The cannon fired its projectile, but did very little damage. Glass fragments covered the porch of the fraternity house next door. The recoil kicked the cannon backwards through the French doors of the boys' fraternity house. Police arrived and in no time had solved the crime. The boys were locked up in the local police station. On Monday morning they were brought to see Dean Tate, renowned on campus as an ultra-strict disciplinarian.

Dean Tate roared into his usual tirade for about ten minutes, then calmed into a state of seriousness to offer his solution to the problem. With the blessing of the chief of police, he demanded that boys pay all damages to both fraternity houses. They would clean and polish the canon so that it would shine as it probably did a hundred years ago. They would bear the cost of transporting the cannon back to Chattanooga and back to its place on Lookout Mountain. Then the boys would select from two alternatives: They could either be prosecuted for the crime *according to local, state, and federal laws; or they could join the Marine Corps.*

The Corps got three good Marines in that deal.

3: Acquiring

Mike Gross, the Thomasville, Georgia, recruiter mentioned in the previous chapter, likes to make his real pitch to the prospect along with his or her family. Sometimes the sale goes quickly; sometimes it takes months. Even after the prospect signs the enlistment agreement, plenty of work remains. Tests, tests, and more tests help to determine whether the applicant is qualified to be a Marine. Not everyone can be one of the Proud, the Few, the Marines. More than that, not everyone can even *apply* to be a Marine.

For those applicants Mike feels are suitable, he arranges a trip to the Sixth Marine Corps Recruiting Region in Jacksonville, Florida. At Jacksonville, the candidate is given a complete medical examination. If a match is found, he or she is sworn in and given a date to report to boot camp.

Is this a costly process? Mike estimates that the financial outlay to put one recruit aboard the bus to boot camp is about $5000. A lot of money, you say? Sure, but the Corps wants only *A Few Good Men and Women,* not just any Tom, Dick, Harry, or Jane that wanders into the recruiting office. Those Few Good Men and Women could be the difference one day in our very existence as a free country. Let's hope we never have to have that bake sale

A Few Good Memories

to continue to pick and to train good men and women to satisfy this country's survival needs.

Did you ever notice how some people know everything about everything? That fact almost cost Hannah M. a wonderful experience. Hannah was nearing high school graduation in April of 1983. Here is her story of how she became a Marine:

I lived with my mom and dad in a little town in Alabama in 1983. I was 18 years old, and I didn't know what I wanted to do. College would cost a lot of money. But, even if I chose college, I still didn't know what I wanted to do. Lots of my friends seemed to know, but not me. I was frustrated.

One day at school I saw this Marine recruiter sitting in the library. He looked so good in his blues. Really good. I went over and sat down. Wow, did he look good! We talked for a while and he gave me some brochures to look over.

I read those brochures. About a week later I looked him up. This time it wasn't because he was so good-looking, but I wanted more information.

All my friends hung out at the skating rink. They started kidding me. "The Marine Corps is too tough. You can't make it," they'd say. They really got on my case about it.

Finally, I had enough. I signed up. Then they started saying things like, "You'll be sorry," and "Been nice knowing you."

Yep. Boot camp was tough. I did things I never thought I could do. But graduation finally came around. My mom and dad were there and they were proud of me. ***And for the first time in my life I was proud of myself!***

I got home from Parris Island on a Saturday. That night I put on my uniform and went to the skating rink. I have never seen a bunch of kids crowd around anybody like they did around me. They wanted to know everything I did, where I was going, and how much money I made. I had them eating out of my hand. I have no doubt that every one of those kids was jealous and would have traded places with me in a second.

I'm an attorney now. I used my GI Bill to go to college. I thank the Corps for giving me this opportunity. And to those kids out there now, hearing all that "You'll be sorry" stuff, just remember: They don't know. Ask them if they've been to boot camp. Tell them to remember the old saying, "Speak not about what you know little."

William B. says that for the first 19 years of his life he lived in fear of having to speak aloud to groups of people. Read his story:

I lived in dread of when I might have to say something in front of a group of people. In high school, we had to give reports. Before it was my time, I'd break out in sweats. When I was up in front, I could hear my voice trembling. This only made it worse. I would lie awake at night and wonder if this was the way I'd go through life. I tried all sorts of remedies. Sometimes my classmates would kid me unmercifully. I couldn't even ask a girl for a date.

Two days before my 19th birthday, I graduated from high school and started looking for a job. Sometimes I'd start to sweat when I was going for an interview. I feel sure I didn't get some of those jobs because I was so nervous. I finally decided I was going to join the Army or the Air Force or something, because I didn't think I'd have to be in front of people.

I ended up joining the Marines. And I was right—I didn't have to stand up in front of a group very much; but when I did, the DI made it happen so fast I didn't think about it. But read on. It wasn't actually the DI that changed me.

When I got home from Parris Island, I went to see James, my buddy. James told me that he was going to a party at the Canteen, and lots of our old friends would probably be there.

I wore my uniform. I was proud that I'd made PFC out of boot camp. It made me feel so good to look down and see that stripe! As soon as we walked in the Canteen, they started crowding around and slapping me on the back and singing the Marine Hymn. One of my old buddies jokingly asked me if my stripe meant I was a general. A couple of the girls from my old class came up and gave me a hug.

Everybody started asking questions about the Marines. They asked what kind of rifle I shot and was it hard to learn to march. Everything. I began to feel that I was important. I started answering those questions like I'd talked to people all my life, and I didn't even realize it.

Now, I'm not saying the Marine Corps training taught me how to talk to people. I've thought about it and realize that what Marine Corps training did was give me confidence to feel as good as anybody I was standing next to. Betsy, one of the nicest girls in our senior class, was there at the Canteen that night. I asked her out and had two dates with her while I was on leave. I ended up marrying her a year later and we're now spending our 32nd year together as husband and wife.

4: Waiting

The moment recruits sign on the dotted lines, the hype hits. They're ready. They're eager. But these new would-be warriors don't always leave the warmth of their homes immediately for Parris Island or San Diego. Sometimes they must wait as much as two or more months for an open class, depending on the backlog. This is good for the recruit, but not always good for the community.

Wesley H. graduated from high school in a little town near Columbia in the Midlands area of South Carolina. He wanted to join the Corps immediately. It was 1965. He was only 17, but he was ready. Here is his story:

> *I wasn't sure I really wanted to join the Marine Corps. I'd talk to my friends about it, and they would give me the old sing-song, "You'll be sorry." Now I look back, and I think that drove me a little harder. I finally made my decision. Why not? I said to myself. I started hunting*

A Few Good Memories

down the recruiter that had visited our school. I found him in Columbia.

I spent a lot of time over in Columbia before I ever picked up the fountain pen. For one thing, I was only 17. I had to get my parents' approval. I wasn't worried about my dad, but I wasn't sure my mom would agree. So, I waited. Two months after my 18th birthday, I graduated from high school, suppressed my nerves, went to the recruiter, and told him I was ready.

I felt good about it. I could imagine myself slaying all sorts of dragons while pretty young girls swooned over me. I was ready to hop the bus that afternoon. Then he told me I'd have a two-month wait.

I got this job as a helper at the Chevrolet dealership. I was pretty good with fixing cars; and, anyway, I needed some money until I left for Parris Island. I tried to get some of my buddies to join, but all they'd do was kid me about what boot camp was like.

One of those buddies was this rich kid named Howard. His family had a river house. Adults used it for weekend parties, which teenagers weren't allowed to attend. The house was about ten miles from town, and it was only used maybe a half-dozen times a year.

But, unknown to Howard's family, we used it a lot. Once in a while (it soon got to be two or three times a week), we'd take a couple of kegs to "Firebase One," as we began to call it. We had heard the term, "firebase," on the news about the war in Vietnam.

Sometimes a carload of girls would drop in. Lots of our friends found out about it and pretty soon the place would get real crowded. After a few beers and everybody singing the Marine Corps Hymn to the top of our lungs, I was satisfied I had done the right thing. Few of us knew all the words to the Hymn, but we'd hum when we got to those parts. A real blast!

All this partying made the time fly by, and soon it was only a week before I was to head to Beaufort, South Carolina, the last stop before the Big Red Gate. Howard *suggested that we have one more humongous party on Saturday night before I left on Monday. I think every kid in three counties came. It started about 3:00 p.m. By 7:00 p.m. there must have been 50 or more kids there. And it was a small town. The beer was disappearing like water over a dam.*

Cars kept arriving. We didn't think about checking them out. Suddenly, about 10:30 that night, the doorway to the log cabin house opened and who should be standing there but Howard's father and one of the county's two sheriff deputies. Kids scattered like leaves in a hurricane. I'd never seen a room empty like that one did. In no more than a couple of minutes every car in the yard was headed down the long half-mile driveway toward River Road, then north back toward town. It looked like the George Washington Bridge in D.C. at five o'clock on Friday afternoon.

My buddy, Gene, and I dived out of the kitchen window and ran to my car. I didn't wait for the driveway traffic to clear. I took the "woods route," missing trees by inches and crushing bushes along the way.

We made it to River Road, but I turned left in a southerly direction because we felt that the other sheriff deputy would be hauling everybody in on the road back to town.

It kind of worked. We did make it back to town, but as we came down Broad Street, the beer had dulled my senses so that I couldn't tell a parking place from a 1959 Chevrolet. I rammed smack into the back of one and crushed its trunk lid.

It turned out the car belonged to Mr. Smith, my boss at the Chevrolet dealership. Mr. Smith had been a Marine during World War II and made landings at Guadalcanal and Iwo. He had two Purple Hearts and a bunch of other ribbons. He was one of the few people on earth that witnessed, firsthand, the actual raising of the flag on Iwo Jima.

A Few Good Memories

I called Mr. Smith. "Don't call the police," he said. "I'll be there in a minute." When he got there, he told me that the damage would be about $125. I said I'd give him ten dollars a month. He agreed, but added, "You graduate from boot camp and keep your nose clean, and then come back and let's talk about it."

The first thing I did after graduation was to go back home to visit. I put on my uniform that sported the PFC stripe that I earned out of boot camp and went to see Mr. Smith. He shook my hand and congratulated me for earning my stripe. I told him I'd be going up to Camp Geiger at Camp Lejeune for infantry training. I handed him my first three payments—three ten-dollar bills.

Mr. Smith stuffed them back in my pocket. "Son," he said, "you got a long road ahead of you. From what I can see, this country is getting deeper into that thing in Southeast Asia. It may be worse than Korea. Your bill is paid. You make this town and the Corps proud."

Wesley's story relates a series of events in his life that has probably been duplicated thousands of times over the years. Wherever there are young Marines, there will be old Marines looking at them longingly, and with envy, and with a sense of pride so deep that it could send chills up and down your spine. It's a fact. I know!

Can the ball continue to roll? Will upcoming generations hold onto this patriotic spirit? Sometimes we wonder. Looking at the six o'clock news, we tend to get the feeling that many young men and women who should be rising to the occasions seem to be falling into the chasm that helps drive this nation further into the depths of tribulation.

Then I recall conversations between my grandfathers and my father and the family. I heard the same concerns from them so many years ago. I remember their admonishments that I should strive to be the best I could in whatever I attempted. Maybe I didn't reach the levels that they had hoped, but I was a Marine. I served my country with honor. That means a lot. I hope that they would have been proud. I have come to believe that in every generation there will be those who do rise to the occasion and serve with honor. All won't be Marines, of course. All *can't* be Marines. It takes someone special to be a Marine.

Maybe some day a microbiologist will invent a medicine that will terminate the aging process—but only for those who serve their country faithfully, Marines or not.

5: The Beginning

Male recruits east of the Mississippi train at Parris Island. Male recruits from the West are sent to the Recruit Training Depot at San Diego. At the present time, all female recruits are trained at Parris Island.

Herbert B. joined the Corps and went through Parris Island in 1950. The Corps has changed from Herb's time, but read his story. It represents what new recruits faced when they arrived at Boot Camp in those days.

On December 22, 1950, I was in a small group from Florida, on a train heading north to Parris Island for USMC boot camp. We stopped at Yemassee, a small town near "the land that God forgot" to wait for people from another train. It was due to get there a couple of days later.

DIs got us off the train by yelling and screaming about how much shit we were, and they never saw such scumbags as we were. They ordered us outside and told us

A Few Good Memories

to form up at attention. I couldn't do it right, so one of them whacked me with a swaggerstick. Man that hurt!

One kept yelling, "What is it about MOVE you don't understand, assholes? Don't you maggots understand f--king English?"

Then they moved us into this ramshackle building they called a barracks. We were put to work swabbing and dusting and painting. They even made us pull grass outside, which there was none of because it was the dead of winter. I was glad two days later when the other train got there and we could leave those sadistic devils behind.

But what I didn't realize was that it was just the beginning. We were met by an even more cruel group of DIs when we hit Parris Island. They had even bigger swaggersticks. They wanted us to move even faster. They liked us even less.

Our DI, SSgt Dixon, was a veteran of lots of battles in the South Pacific. He was as tough as nails, but, to his credit, he treated everybody in a fair manner. His assistant DI was a young corporal who was probably jealous of SSgt Dixon's war record, so he took it out on us in his own way. Nothing was fair about him. He seemed to get after whichever one of us was in his way. He'd go to the slop chute at night and get all beered up, then come back about 1:00 a.m., and roust us out. Sometimes he'd blow his beer breath in our faces and chide us about us not being able to have a beer. He was a mean snake, to say the least. We hated—really hated—that SOB.

It's different nowadays. Recruits on the East Coast arrive by plane in Charleston, South Carolina, and await further transportation to Parris Island. Recruits west of the Mississippi River fly to San Diego, California.

Recruits about to enter boot camp are herded into a waiting area by Marine Corps handlers. The umbilical cord connects. Recruits become the property of the Corps. Recruits eat their first government meal, usually from the counter of the airport diner.

A Few Good Memories
_____

Handlers watch over them like a mother hen, because most have no idea of the meaning of discipline.

The recruits' orders are checked to be sure they are where they should be. Heaven help the boot that shows up without that set of orders.

The following story is submitted by a former Marine, Bobby L., who did lose his orders, but came out of it smelling like a rose:

Right after I joined up in 1987, I was excited. But, as the time grew near to report to Parris Island, I got nervous and frightened. Even so, I was eager to get started and to get on with it.

I wanted to be a Marine. My friends at home told me I would never make it. Sure, I lived in a big city—New York—one of the biggest cities in the world. I had never been in the woods much, but I vowed to be a good Marine. I would be a tough Marine. I would make my DI happy.

On the day before I left, I kept checking my orders. I made sure to pack only what I was told to bring—nothing more or less. My dad and mom and little sister drove me to the airport to catch the 7:20 early morning plane toward Charleston, South Carolina. My orders said government ground transportation would take me from Charleston to the Parris Island Recruit Depot.

I shook my dad's hand and gave my mom and little sister a hug. I would soon begin my Marine Corps tour of duty. It sounded good. Underneath my fear, I felt proud.

The Delta aircraft lifted off from La Guardia and headed south. Flight attendants gave me some pastry and orange juice. I looked at this as my first meal as a Marine. I thought I was already a Marine.

The plane landed in Washington for a twenty-minute stop, then it was off again toward Atlanta. I snoozed nervously, and then woke up in a start, thinking I'd better brush up on what I was to do at the Charleston

A Few Good Memories

airport. I'd read it a hundred times, but decided to read it once more for good measure.

I looked around my seat for my orders. Where are my orders? They've got to be here. I looked in, around, over, and under, but I couldn't find that manila packet. Did I leave it at La Guardia? The orders must be here.

I went back a few seats; forward a few seats. I crawled around the deck and looked under the seats. The other passengers must have thought I was nuts. A Catholic priest felt sorry for me when I told him my problem. Soon, the two of us were crawling around the cabin like a couple of rats.

I couldn't believe it. I remembered having my orders in my hand when I left. (I think). My mom had kept reminding me.

The inevitable doubt-syndrome set in. Did I really have them when I boarded? Perspiration poured down my face. I told the flight attendant my plight. She went to the cockpit and talked with the pilots. After an eternity, she came back and said that they had sent a message to La Guardia to see if I'd left the packet on the counter. Fifteen minutes went by. The attendant returned with bad news. They couldn't find them.

What now? I thought. What's going to happen to me when I tell the Marines I lost my orders? They'll eat me alive.

Then, somebody up there was with me. As we made our approach into Washington, the flight attendant rushed up to my seat and said that they had received a message. My mother had found my orders in the car exactly where I had left them. They were being sent on another plane to Charleston. I was to check in at the Delta counter around 6:00 p.m. I breathed again and enjoyed the flight to Atlanta.

A plane change in Atlanta put me on the short flight to Charleston. But my imagination came alive again. I began to think. What if the orders don't make it to Charleston? What if they go to Charleston, West Virginia?

A Few Good Memories

What if somebody goofs like I did? Why did I ever join the Corps?

We landed in Charleston about 3:00 p.m. With three hours to wait, I decided to walk off my nervousness. I saw a big sign that read "Transportation to Parris Island." Standing beside the sign was a really ugly Marine who was at least twelve feet tall and weighed somewhere around seven hundred pounds. He had stripes from his shoulder down to his elbow. Beside him in a huddle were some scared-looking young males, no doubt headed for boot camp.

I ducked behind a big sign and escaped to the snack area. For hours, I hid and waited and sweated it out. The clock ticked closer to 6:00 p.m. I became more scared. Things hadn't gone too well since 7:20 this morning, and I was sure something else would get screwed up.

At 6:00 p.m., I went to the Delta counter just in time to hear my name announced over the scratchy PA system. A big smile lit up the lady's face when I told her who I was. I could have kissed her. Maybe another day. Right now I had my orders. I took a huge, badly needed breath.

I found the "Transportation to Parris Island" sign and reported in to that big ugly Marine. He grunted and pointed me to a waiting room where I waited and waited. About 10:00 p.m. another big, ugly Marine had taken over. He herded us into the bus toward Parris Island. And it was just beginning.

When a load is collected, the bus starts the two-hour ride to Parris Island. The new recruits are herded inside. Orders are checked. Recruits are accounted for and the bus leaves Charleston for Parris Island. They arrive at "Receiving" a little after midnight.

Bus-driver Jack O., one of the civilian contract bus drivers I interviewed, said he been driving this run for over a year. He told this story:

A Few Good Memories

A military policeman sometimes goes with the new drivers to keep the noise to a dull roar. Every load of recruits follows just about the same ritual. At first the recruits are all loud and happy. They start singing the Marine Corps Hymn. The whole group chimes in. It gets louder.

As our bus gets nearer to Beaufort, the singing dies down. Suddenly the Red Gate appears. It's an awesome sight. It's the entrance to Parris Island. When the recruits ask me about it, all I tell them is, "One way in, one way out."

The guard at the kiosk checks our papers and waves us through. We travel a mile-long causeway surrounded by threatening tidewater marshes. Recruits press their heads hard against the windows. They stare at the scary quagmire on either side. It's an awesome sight, made even more awesome by the running lights of our bus, and sometimes a full moon. I swear I can hear a pin drop. Sometimes recruits start whispering about alligators or snakes.

We reach the end of the causeway and pass under a huge canopy formed by dozens of two-hundred-year-old live oak trees. Each one of those trees is a magnificent product of nature. As we pass under this canopy, it's such an eerie and weird sensation. I tell the recruits to listen up. I tell them they can almost hear the ghosts of thousands of Marines cheering. It's those who have tread this path before, and have gone on to give their lives while "fighting our nations battles" at Tripoli, in World War I, World War II, Korea, Vietnam, and every battle that the Corps has ever fought.

Six minutes later our bus pulls in to "Receiving." It's about 0030 hours; thirty minutes after midnight. I open the bus door and a big, tough-looking Marine climbs aboard with a smirk on his face and a welcome from the commanding general. Then he explains three rules of military law that affect recruits at this stage of the game. Rule I forbids military persons from being anywhere except where they are supposed to be, or UA (unauthorized absence). Rule II prohibits disobedience of a lawful order. Rule III says that proper respect must be shown to all officers. The recruits are all eyes. They huddle together.

And I remember this. I may be a civilian bus driver now, but I went through boot camp at Parris Island once and I know the drill.

It's time to disembark. It's time to begin the long, hard road to becoming a Marine—a task that, statistically speaking, only 84 percent of these recruits will achieve.

A Few Good Memories

6: Receiving

Receiving. Sounds a bit like the back door of the Winn-Dixie grocery store, doesn't it? But that's its function. Every recruit passes through Receiving before seeing the light of day.

Frank B. remembers his encounter with Receiving in this way:

It was April of 1979. When I heard the brakes hiss and felt the bus screech to a halt, I knew we were there. Except for a few outside lights, I couldn't see a thing. It was eerie. So dark. This Marine sergeant climbed aboard the bus and demanded absolute silence. "On behalf of the commanding general of the Recruit Training Depot," he said, "I want to welcome you to Parris Island."

Then some wise ass named Baker countered with, "Hey, Sarge. How come he never come over and told us hisself?"

That lit off the sergeant. In all the years that have passed since, I doubt Baker has ever wise-cracked again. Throughout the night, every time we stood in line waiting,

A Few Good Memories

Baker was scrubbing and rescrubbing anything and everything with a toothbrush. Once he told the sergeant that he was finished with the baseboard. "Think so? Scrub it again. When you finish that, start on something else. If you can't find nothing else, start all over."

The sergeant noticed a couple of recruits looking over at Baker and snickering a bit. He brought some more toothbrushes and put them to scrubbing the chairs around the room. "We got plenty of toothbrushes back in Supply," he said. "Enough for everybody." From then on, nobody even cast a glance at Baker or his two helpers.

Having been well briefed on the purpose of the more than 60 sets of yellow footprints painted on the deck outside Receiving, recruits pile off the bus, plant their feet on one of the 45-degree angle yellow prints on the sidewalk, and adjust their posture as close to attention as they can imagine.

After an interminable wait, probably designed to create bewilderment, recruits are rushed inside to a large assembly room with schoolroom-type chairs. The recruits are already exhausted. It has been a long day so far. But this day is far from over. And heaven help any recruit who sits in those chairs before receiving permission.

Miles T. remembered how exhausted he was in 1984 when he arrived at Receiving:

We were standing in the yellow footprints when the gunnery sergeant sent us running on the double to the building and into the first hatch (doorway) on the right. When we entered the room, I saw it was filled with old schoolroom chairs. I picked out a good seat, front and center, and sat down. Why not? That's the way I did last year at school.

My mistake. I learned a lesson: A recruit sits only when and where he is told to sit. I did chair lifts for at least an hour, seemed like more. In fact, for the next twelve

A Few Good Memories

weeks, all of us learned that we weren't supposed to do anything except what and when we were told. "You belong to the Corps now," the DI said. "We tell you when to eat, what to eat, when to bathe, when to shave, when to crap, and when to breathe. You do nothing unless we tell you. And you do everything we tell you."

I had used up my allotment of "chair time," according to the gunnery sergeant, so I had to do my paperwork standing up. All I wanted to do was sleep.

In fact, recruits don't sleep at all the first night. About 33 hours pass from the time they reach Receiving until they are allowed to close their eyes. They fill out forms for an hour. And just let a male recruit show up wearing earrings. Ten minutes later he'll wish he'd never seen an earring. Marine Corps sergeants love earrings, but only on pretty ladies. They will make that point in dramatic ways.

Lowell U. was one of the new breed of male youngsters with pierced ears. He remembers very well how Marine staff sergeants little appreciate these decorative additions:

At the urging of my girlfriend, I had had my left ear pierced when I was a junior in high school. The next year, 1976, I graduated when thousands of men were coming back after Vietnam. Jobs were a little scarce, especially for somebody just out of high school. Also, I guess it was especially bad for somebody with a green four-leaf clover hanging out of his left ear.

So I went to see this Marine recruiter I met when I was in high school. I made sure to take my earring out every time I saw him. I finally decided to make the move and join the Corps.

I forgot all about that earpiece on the way to Parris Island. But that was the first thing the staff sergeant saw when he herded us off the bus. He made me take the earring out and put it in a bag and then put that bag inside another bag and hand it to him. He said he wouldn't dare dirty his hands by touching female jewelry that had been worn by a man.

Then he made me walk around swinging my hips and talking like a female. He kept yelling that my voice wasn't high enough. Soon I was talking in small squeaks and parading around in circles. All the other recruits were getting quite a kick out of it.

I thought the end was finally near. It wasn't. He handed me the bag and I had to take out the earring and drop it on the concrete deck. Then he handed me a hammer and made me beat the pin into a fine powder.

After filling out all those forms, the classic moment of the night arrives. Male recruits line up in a passageway (hallway) near three chairs. Standing beside these three chairs are three men in white suits, smiling. They look like doctors with scalpels in their hands, but these men are barbers. One by one, recruits are ordered to sit in one of the chairs. The barbers know one style—shaved. Some recruits can't help but make little cracks like, "Taper the back and leave full sideburns." For those reading this, especially for those who might go to boot camp one day, don't say stupid things like that.

This is the quickest haircut these male recruits have ever known. Thirty seconds. Thirty-five max. If their friends back home could see them now. A free haircut. At least no tip. (Don't make the tip joke either.)

Female recruits get a haircut also, except it's not a head shave. They are clipped down to about three inches. On one of my visits to Parris Island, I watched a female recruit, bearing long and curly and very pretty blonde hair, take her seat. In less than a minute, those long blonde curls formed a pile three inches deep. When the recruit got up from the chair, she looked down at her hair, grabbed at her hair, and burst into tears. The female staff sergeant handler expressed no sympathy.

At about 0130, 32 hours of heavy activity remain before sack time. Recruits must turn in all extraneous items such as

A Few Good Memories

cigarette lighters, knives, key chains, money, even jewelry—anything not needed in the conduct of boot camp. Every item with a serial number is registered and placed in a sack. The recruit and a DI will sign two copies of a document attesting to the contents. The recruit gets one copy. One stays in the files. Recruits will have this sack returned at graduation or ELS (Entry Level Separation, meaning he or she is one of the 16 percent who didn't make it).

Then, recruits pass through the supply line and draw personal gear—toothbrush, toothpaste, soap, towels, bath cloths, and by all means deodorant. They draw uniforms. Then it's through the war gear line. This includes a poncho, a pack, a canteen, a field jacket, and 50 more individual items. The recruit signs a receipt for this 782 gear on a Form (what else) 782. Having been aboard the base for only a couple of hours, the recruit is already into the Corps for over $1200.

The hands of the 24-hour clock now point to about 0400. The chow lines are opened for the recruits' first official Marine Corps meals in the chow hall. With bright metal chow trays pressed firmly against their chests, recruits approach the steaming hot tables. Some recruits feel just too tired to eat. But eat they must. They may take as much as they want, but not one scrap of food is to be dumped through the tray window. Not now. Not later. Not ever.

Then it's shower time. Gone are the 30-minute-long civilian showers, where the water runs so long and hot that parents think it's costing a week's salary for the kid to take a bath. Here, recruits learn to take a Marine Corps shower. From the overhead, shower rings hang down the entire length of the shower area. Pull one and water squirts from the nozzles. Release it and it stops. Ingenious, right? The idea is to soak for five seconds, release the ring, soap for 30 seconds (all over), then pull the ring and rinse for ten seconds. Perfect. The recruit is as clean as a whistle—in 45 seconds flat!

For the first time, recruits begin to look the part. It's time to don the uniform they'll wear for the next three to four to six years or even longer. Each recruit's civilian clothes items are stored in a sack. That is, all clothes except underwear and socks.

These are burned to ashes in the incinerator. Who'd want those smelly things back after 12 weeks in storage?

After a linen issue, recruits are instructed in making up a rack (bed). Most recruits have never made up a bed in their lives. Mama did it. They learn how to make military corners. They learn how a rack is properly made: tight as a drum, no wrinkles, every flap hidden. They also learn that the blanket must fit so tightly that a quarter, when flipped onto the rack, will bounce back into the air. They keep looking at their made-up racks and long to climb in. It won't happen for another 15 hours. It is only 0600 hours. "Lights out" is at 2100 hours, later tonight.

The Corps wastes no time. Next, recruits learn about the insurance option. The cost for a $35,000 policy is less than $3.00 per month. The government subsidizes the remainder. Any recruit who rejects this coverage should have his head examined.

The clock on the bulkhead (wall) approaches 0700. Recruits huddle in a room for a heart-to-heart talk with their staff sergeant handler. They read a document that allows them to swear that all the answers on their enlistment application were true. These are questions like drug use, problems with the law, and age. This is "fess up, come clean" time. If they sign this document and it is later found to be false, they are subject to immediate release, and in some cases, federal fraud charges.

Recruits must also answer questions about their treatment thus far at boot camp. They will be asked whether they have been improperly treated or called inappropriate names since they arrived on base. Any answer in the affirmative temporarily relieves the drill instructor and an investigation gets underway.

Note: During one of my visits to Parris Island, I was honored to have the opportunity to have lunch with seven drill instructors: four male, three female. We talked about the "New Corps" and especially how the days of striking, even touching, a recruit is gone. They explained that a number of times during the 12 weeks, recruits are reminded that they may report, without prejudice, any physical, verbal, or mental abuse by a drill instructor.

During Drill Instructor School, DIs are instructed, day in and day out, in the philosophy of boot camp and the New Corps. Part of this instruction is that abuse serves no purpose and will not be tolerated. This teaching continues during boot camp. It becomes second-nature that a drill instructor never strikes or touches a recruit except in helping to correct rifle-shooting positions, close-order drill positions, and the like.

If a recruit reports such an abuse, the drill instructor is temporarily relieved of duty and an investigation begins. The Corps is careful to ensure that such a charge has substantial evidence. Fellow recruits are invited to testify, without prejudice, as to any knowledge of an offense.

The Corps understands that, in spite of the excellent training and tight control, once in a great while a drill instructor might be guilty of going a bit too far. The Corps also understands that sometimes a recruit, who can't handle the discipline of boot camp, will conjure up a false accusation. The Corps is competent to get to the bottom of any situation and ferret out the truth.

A drill instructor found to be guilty of violating his or her regulations is permanently relieved from duty and his or her commanding officer will recommend further action. A recruit who is found to have falsely accused a drill instructor is dealt with in a serious manner.

Recruits are asked if they have second thoughts about boot camp, and if so, why. Some will decide that it's too much for them. The Corps, however, having already invested thousands of dollars getting a valuable recruit aboard the base, takes him or her out of training and tries to work toward a solution. The recruit is told that everyone is frightened, that fright is perfectly normal. Most will decide to continue training.

Some recruits insist upon quitting. They are separated from the group and transferred to a special barracks area and are constantly monitored and counseled. If no progress is made within a week or two, the recruit becomes an ELS (Entry Level

A Few Good Memories

Separation). Drill instructors work very hard to dissuade these early drops. The stigma of dropping out or quitting can follow recruits for a long time during their lives. But even if a recruit decides to return to training, he or she is monitored for weeks.

It has been a long day without sleep—33 hours, the longest time most of these young recruits have ever stayed awake at one clip. When taps sounds, they are ready.

But everyone isn't allowed to sleep immediately. At no time in the Corps, be it boot camp or the battlefields of Guadalcanal, will a unit rest or sleep unless watch (sentry) is set. In this case, recruits serve their time at firewatch, two at a time, for an hour each. The firewatch's job is to patrol the area, keeping alert for any sign of danger, such as fire or unauthorized entry to their area.

The temptation is always there to grab a few minutes of secret 'shuteye' while on watch. Recruits have been instructed as to just how serious a matter it is to sleep on watch. Simply hearing the word "court-martial" is frightening enough, but when recruits learn that to go to sleep on watch subjects *them* to the possibility of a court-martial, their eyes pop open and drowsiness seems to disappear. Besides that, drill instructors are known to burst in at any time to check watch.

One of the first lessons that recruits learn in boot camp is that pockets are not to be used. "Stuff" in the pocket makes bulges. These bulges create a poor appearance. Some recruits actually sew their pockets shut.

Howard D. is one of the brave Marines who helped stop the Japanese aggression during WWII. Here is his story:

I enlisted in August of 1941. "If we're going to war, I want to go with the Marines," I kept telling my mama. So they sent me to this place that God forgot, Parris Island.

A few scorching days after I got there, I was wishing I'd never heard of the Marines. It must have been over 100 degrees in the shade and the DIs never let us have any free time.

After finishing chow one evening, we marched back to the squad bay to get ready for another one of those eternal inspections that nobody passes. Guess I forgot, but I jammed my left hand into my trouser pocket.

He got me. The DI chewed on and on about military bearing and how pockets are made to look sharp, not to use.

I played the fool and questioned what was wrong with using my pockets to hold some matches. Well, he didn't take too kindly to that and he got me off to the side and explained it.

My punishment was to fill my pockets with fine, sharp, grimy, cutting, Parris Island sand and to sew the pockets shut. I had to endure the next two weeks like that. Every time I did my washing, I had to tear out the stitches, pour out the sand, wash the trousers, fill them back up with sand, and sew them up.

Even today, fifty years later, I still do not put my hands in my pockets. After all that pocket drill, I certainly believe that the meaning for all of the hassle and the apparently pointless orders made itself known when our battalion landed on Tarawa. Even though my platoon lost over half of its Marines within the first couple hours of battle, it would have been much worse if we had not been trained to obey, obey, obey, and not ask dumb questions, like what is wrong with using your pockets.

7: Getting Started

Prior to week one, boot camp isn't such an all-terrible experience that recruits have expected. They tend to get a little complacent. Sure, a lot of barking of orders has helped in moving them from place to place. But so far, drill instructors haven't been especially tough on recruits.

Week one, however, dawns a new day. Most recruits are in the worst possible physical shape. They've lived off candy bars and fast food hamburgers. Few know the meaning of the word "breakfast." Their primary activity has been lying on Mama's sofa and watching MTV until four in the morning.

One of the chief purposes of week one is a combination of diminishing flab and taking on muscle. At an average 19 years of age, most these young boots can take it. Every day they quick-change into their physical training uniforms—red shorts and yellow jerseys. They prepare for two and a half hours of heavy physical training. It does the trick. Soon, physical change is noticeable. The average loss of a pound of fat per day begins to show up. Every pound of flab per day transforms into a half-pound pound per day of hard-toned muscle and meat. Uniforms fit a bit looser. Bodies slim while seeming to reach for the sky.

A Few Good Memories

In every group of 60 recruits, about nine or ten are overweight and must be watched. One or two might have a minor ailment not bad enough for disqualification but one that must be monitored. They'll wear yellow jerseys but with double red horizontal stripes. They are watched over constantly by the DIs. A recruit showing any sign of exhaustion or sickness is quickly loaded aboard the medical vehicle and gets a fast ride to the base hospital.

Recruits learn to exist. The old saying, "Don't speak until spoken to," is to be followed to the letter. Once in a while a recruit comes along who delights in being funny. He or she, probably has never had much attention, and uses every opportunity to be a clown. It usually happens in the early stages, week one or two.

Lowell J. tells this story:

I was 19 years old when I joined up and went to Parris Island in 1982. I grew up in a small farm town in Missouri. Small was an overstatement. Our high school class consisted of seven boys and six girls. And at that, it was the largest class in the history of the little town.
I had never been to a big city. We went to Springfield on our Senior Class trip, but it was only for two days. The most exciting event of the trip was seeing a modern movie theater with nice soft seats. The seats in our theater back home had springs sticking through the cover. Sometimes our projector operator at home would forget and let a reel run out and we'd have to wait a few minutes for him to load the next reel. I always liked to use that opportunity to make stupid jokes about the people in the audience.
The first week at Parris Island was easier than I thought it would be. We had just received our uniforms and started learning about the Corps and close-order drill. The DIs let me get away with some of my clowning. Sometimes they'd jump on me and make me do pushups and

things like that, but nothing really bad. I thought boot camp would be a breeze. I got brave.

Week one came. We started physical training on a Monday afternoon. I started making smart remarks about this being a snap. I didn't think the DI was hearing me so I kept it up.

Everybody was exhausted at the end of the two-and-a-half-hour session. The DI called us to attention and yelled, "Jackson. Front and center."

I left my position and approached front and center.

"About face," the DI looked at me. Then I was facing my platoon. The DI explained to the platoon that since I had been clowning around about how easy PT was, the whole platoon would be back out on the grass at 1900 hours for another PT period. And we were.

The DI finally brought me front and center and put me go through some extra PT of my own. He kept asking me if this was a snap. I'd answer, "No, sir." He'd say he couldn't hear me.

At the end of that PT session, the whole platoon threatened me with my life if I didn't keep my mouth shut. From that day forward I was a model recruit!

Ron M. was at Parris Island in 1967. He was from South Florida and had enjoyed life for his first 19 years. Ron liked to throw down a brew once in a while, like every night. And, as he said, "Cigarettes go very well with a can of Bud."

Ron learned that in boot camp he couldn't have what he wanted when he wanted it. In fact he rarely could ever have what he wanted at all. And he liked his cigarettes. Here is his story:

My two-pack-per-day smoking habit changed drastically because of the two-joints-per-day limit at Parris Island back then. My platoon was in its third week of training. Like most of the smokers at Parris Island, I craved some long drags from a pack of those weeds that were sitting, unused, in my locker box.

A Few Good Memories

The hardest part was watching drill instructors enjoy their smokes during breaks in the field. They always seemed to light up when we had a clear view of them. No doubt that many of them lit up just to hassle us. To a smoker, this was the highest level of harassment.

One particular morning, our platoon was more dead than alive after the pushups, sit-ups, and the three-mile run—a real *run. We heard S/SGT Ringer shout, "Smokers, fall out!" That was the signal for smokers to form a circle and shout the usual, "Sir, the smoking circle for platoon 281 is now formed, sir!" S/SGT Ringer, apparently being hard of hearing like most other DIs, shouted, "I can't hear you, ladies!"*

We repeated, "Sir, the smoking circle for platoon 281 is now formed, sir!" This continued for at least a dozen times. Finally, the sergeant announced, "The smoking lamp is lit." We lit up and dragged so hard that the red glow of burning cigarettes was probably visible across the grinder. However, the cigarette smoke burned our throats badly because of all the shouting we had done during physical training. I came to the realization that it would be a long time before I'd have a chance to smoke a cigarette in peace.

However, to my surprise, an opportunity came once when I had the 0200 firewatch. My patrol area was the squad bay and the immediate grounds around our barracks. During one pass through the squad bay, I reached in my locker box and grabbed a full pack of Marlboros. I walked my post properly until I reached the dark area near the dumpster. I carefully opened the side hatch of the dumpster and crawled inside.

I lit the first cigarette and pulled the sweet smoke into my lungs. Then I slowly exhaled, and enjoyed the ecstasy. I thought I was in heaven. I finished that cigarette and lit another. And another. I stayed in that dumpster a half hour and chain-smoked half the pack.

During the next round through the squad bay, I stopped at the scuttlebutt (water cooler, which is definitely off-limits to recruits) and gulped down the cold water. Soon it was time to get back to firewatch duty. It was almost 0400 and time for my relief to take over.

After making a quick head call, my watch ended, so I woke up my relief. That short period of rebellion gave me a new perspective and the remainder of my time on the Island went quite well.

One of the Parris Island boots I interviewed during his training said his recruiter from Urbana, Illinois, offered him some advice about how to get along. Humorous it was, but it contained three steps that may be followed not only in boot camp, but throughout the Marine Corps, even life:

Shoot the shit.
Get a receipt.
Move with the largest group.

Chow call is an unforgettable experience. Even though recruits are never denied their three meals, sometimes it's a little hectic. With a maximum of 20 minutes allowed for each meal, hardly enough time to taste, recruits actually do have ample time to gobble down those calories. If they don't, they'll regret it later.

Light conversation is allowed once recruits get to the table, but not in the chow line.

Donald M. went through Parris Island in 1958. He learned not to talk in the chow line:

The chow line, like every place else at Parris Island Boot Camp, is not the place to get caught talking or horsing around. One day, I forgot the rule about talking. Rules are rules, and for a purpose. Can you imagine everybody in a platoon of Marines in combat going off and doing his own thing?

It was 1958. That was when DIs could crack you over the head with those swagger sticks. Our platoon had just started a week before. I'm sure our DI, SSgt Miller, was waiting for a perfect moment to make a point.

His wait was not in vain. It was evening chow and we were moving up the line slowly. I started telling my buddy, Richard, about the night before I left for PI. I told him how my girl friend, Kathy, cried during our entire date; about how I took her to the drive-in theater and was getting away with murder in the back seat of my old '51 Ford. Her mama had never let us go to the drive-in before, but this time we went without telling her. Kathy said I'd be away so long that I deserved some fun.

Suddenly, SSgt. Miller rapped me over the head with his swagger stick. He whacked Richard on the back of his neck with the second blow. He began to chew on us unmercifully. Then he made both of us get up on an empty table and start yelling things like, "I'm 150 pounds of death, disaster, and destruction. Ain't no swabbie ever been born that can take us."

Then he made us sing the Marine Corps Hymn, first together, then solo. This went on for a few minutes. The crowning blow was when Miller made us stand on that table and repeat the conversation we were having when he caught us. The guys in our platoon clapped as we described in detail what I was doing with Kathy in the back seat. Things I'd never done before.

I never opened my mouth in the chow line again. Not even when I got to Camp Lejeune and was assigned to the Sixth Marines. It didn't hurt me. I think it made a better, more disciplined Marine out of me.

In fact, I don't even talk in lines at bank teller windows today for fear that Miller is hiding around the corner.

Every second of every day at least one drill instructor is with the recruits. They are never alone. Up until this point in boot camp, all the DIs have done is make noise. Stand by, mates. The worst is yet to come.

A Few Good Memories
───────────────

For three weeks, boots will be in Phase I training. They'll work very hard in the classroom learning Marine Corps history, studying the Marine Corps Guidebook, learning to drill, and how to dress. They'll learn when to speak and when not to speak. These days are especially tough.

It's an impossible task to select recruits and score a 100-percent success rate. Some recruits start looking for a way out. They remember the marshland tides that they passed on the way in. Most of them know they don't want to try to escape that way. The best way for these below-grade recruits to get out is to try to quit. A few do, and they'll use any means possible.

This is my own story of how the Corps handles disabled, injured, or sick recruits:

> *In December of 1999, on one of my visits to Parris Island for research for this book, Gunnery Sergeant Blake and Staff Sergeant Williams escorted me through the MRP (Medical Rehabilitation Platoon) building. At MRP, certain recruits are housed for recovery and observation. They might be injured or sick. Or they might simply have a negative mental attitude toward training. Gunny Blake cautioned me to expect anything as we walked through the squad bays.*
>
> *In the first squad bay, we came upon two recruits. One had a cast on his right arm. He was pressing his uniform with his left. The other recruit sat at attention in a wheel chair in a full-body brace. He had stopped shining his military-issue shoes.*
>
> *Both recruits shouted in a very military and respectful manner, "Good afternoon, sirs." Since non-recruits do not talk to recruits, we walked through without comment.*
>
> *We continued into a smaller squad bay. "Those two back there were valid rehab cases," said Gunny Blake. "This is the sad one." A recruit sat hunched down, over a footlocker, bawling at the top of his lungs. It wasn't mere*

sniffle. It was a serious cry. He cried the kind of tears you'd spill if the world were five minutes from ending and you had just met the girl of your dreams.

"What's the matter, Gunny?" I asked. "He miss his mama?"

"Yes, sir," answered Gunny Blake. "That's exactly it."

The gunny and I kept on walking while SSgt Williams remained with the crying recruit. It was disturbing.

When we finished our tour, I questioned GySgt Blake about the recruit. "What'll you do? Send him home?"

"No, sir. This is unusual. But we won't let him quit, not yet anyway. We couldn't do that to him. The doctors say this will probably pass. We'll try to make a Marine out of him." Then the gunny added more emphatically, "We don't want to send him home like this. He'd be ruined for life. We'll keep working with him until the doctors tell us to give up. SSgt. Williams does his hourly visit. That's at the direction of the doctors. We'll bring him around."

I was very impressed with the Corps' take on this issue. What could be more kind, if even by Marines? "Ruined for life," the gunny had said. The Corps has a heart. I was impressed.

Six weeks later I went back to Parris Island. I made a point of looking up GySgt Blake. I was happy to learn that the homesick recruit had shed his previous state of mind. He had been transferred to a different platoon and was doing well. I was proud that I could count myself among the Few, the Proud, the Marines.

Reveille on a Marine Corps base is a command to wake up and start the day. When the bugle sounds, unless you're authorized to sleep in, you'd better plant your tootsies on the deck. In boot camp it is especially important for recruits to learn this. DIs make a point of being sure of that.

A Few Good Memories
───────────────

Roger T., a San Diego recruit during the early eighties, submitted this story:

Recruit Norman was one of the fifty-six members of our San Diego recruit platoon. During his previous eighteen years, growing up in Seattle, he'd probably never gotten up before eight o'clock.

We tried to help him. It would help us if we could. Every morning when the reveille sounded, we'd roll him out, drag him to the head, and revive him to the point that he could get himself started. We knew that when Norman got in trouble, the whole platoon got in trouble.

Marines learn to help one other, but this was ridiculous. We got tired of coddling the lazy bum. One night, we decided we were through, no matter whether it hurt us or not. The next morning, the whistle sounded. Fifty-five of us scurried to police up our area, shave, shower, and head for morning formation. Norman snored away in his sack. I sort of felt sorry for the poor guy, but he was going to have to learn.

At roll call, Sgt. Hanks looked around. "Norman," he yelled. Instead of the usual, "Sir, Recruit Norman here, sir," a deathly silence hung over our area.

"Where's Norman?" Sgt. Hanks bellowed.

"Sir, Recruit Norman is still in the sack, sir," answered one of the brave souls in the platoon. That sent Hanks into absolute orbit.

When a military unit is under command, the officer or NCO in charge never abandons his command. He will turn it over to another qualified person. Not this time. Sgt. Hanks spun off toward the squad bay, seeming to leave a rooster tail of dust in his wake.

We heard yelling in the squad bay. We heard a metal GI can slam into a wall locker. We heard Hanks rocking Norman's rack, continuously slamming the four legs onto the deck. It sounded like an old Browning

Automatic Rifle, from back in the sixties, set on automatic fire.

In minutes, Norman came running out toward the formation, shoes in one hand, uniform in the other. Sgt. Hanks followed on his heels. It was a funny sight with him trying to dress as fast as he could.

"You have one minute to get squared away," Sgt. Hanks yelled at the maggot. He was dressing so quickly that it seemed that both boondockers went on at the same time.

The DI was not finished. "Prepare for inspection," he commanded. The inspection consisted of Sgt. Hanks standing directly in front of Norman, calling out discrepancies. "No belt. No socks. No skivvy shirt. Shoelaces untied. Not shaved. No cover (hat)."

Boot camp is a learning experience. Norman learned from this that he must get up at the first blast of the whistle. He turned into a good, squared-away recruit.

During the last week of boot camp, when things calmed down and the DIs began to take on more of a fatherly role, we sat around in a circle while Sgt. Hanks talked to us. He recalled that day. "Norman," he said, "nobody expects you guys to come in perfect. What we try to do is to get you where you are today."

8: The Corps Means Business

During the early weeks of boot camp, recruits are pushed hard physically. Retired M/Sgt McNeil, a former DI from Parris Island, sent a story to me explaining a formula that he developed, which proves that every recruit platoon loses an entire recruit during the first week of training and no one misses the recruit. Actually, everybody was happy. Here is his theory:

A recruit platoon contains about 60 recruits. The average recruit coming into boot camp weighs about 180 pounds. During the first week, the average recruit loses about three pounds. Therefore, 60 recruits times 3 pounds equals 180 pounds; in other words, the weight of one recruit. Now where did that recruit go? No one cares. Nobody misses him (or her). In fact, this makes everybody happy for this loss.

M/Sgt McNeil's creative deduction is a humorous explanation of the seriousness of the Corps in creating physically conditioned men out of whatever comes through the Big Red Gate.

A Few Good Memories

The first weeks of recruit training are dedicated to bringing 60 people up to a common denominator of fitness. From there, they'll launch the effort to complete the job and make these men into Marines.

Week two could be called "weed-out week." By now, two or three recruits have decided that Boot Camp is not the life for them. They'd rather drop out, go home and waste their life away on the street corners, watch MTV, eat pogey bait and drink soda pop or even something stronger. Drill instructors want every recruit to graduate, but they'd rather get rid of non-Marine material early. They'd rather not, and will not, have goof-offs holding the good ones back.

No, the Corps is not for everyone. In fact, it's for a very few. Boot Camp is a super-test; one that determines which of these civilians can clear those demanding hurdles and be one of the very best. Drill instructors push recruits especially hard in the early days. They test, test, and test to see how recruits react under every kind of situation. This is the time to weed out the non-Marines. When a landing craft under heavy enemy artillery fire is on the way in to the enemy shoreline, it's too late to discover that some Marine just cracked.

Another two or three recruits would like to be Marines but just don't have what it takes. Not only must a recruit be physically strong, but he or she must be psychologically and mentally powerful as well. One or two recruits will be physically tough enough but won't be able to take the emotional stress. It's damning on the sanity of a marginal recruit to spend two hours cleaning a rifle, and then have the DI send him or her to the pits because of a dirty weapon.

For those motivated recruits not physically up to par, remedial training may help. The senior drill instructor may decide to remove these recruits from the training platoon to an organized physical conditioning schedule under the watchful eye of an especially trained drill instructor. This drill instructor's job is to beef up recruits in minimum time.

A Few Good Memories

Some recruits are mentally unfit. U.S. Navy doctors control their schedules and recommend when the recruits may either go back to duty or be sent to ELS (Early Level Separation).

Recruits, in their own minds, condemn DIs for such elevated expectations as to the would-be Marines' abilities to drill with perfection by week 2. Actually, this is not true. DIs understand that the combination of sweat and time and practice is what brings perfection. Every session on the grinder brings about a new and more difficult close-order drill movement, making previous maneuvers more understandable and second-nature.

Perceptive minds of drill instructors observe when morale of the platoon is dropping. They know why. It happens in every platoon in recruit training. Just as the saying goes that one bad apple spoils the barrel, so it is in the Corps and life in general. But the Corps won't have bad apples. One or two recruits in every platoon may end up as troublemakers, or slouches. They can't take it. They won't accept the discipline and order that it takes to become a Marine. It's time to rattle cages, lest it spread.

Vernon F., retired Marine and former drill instructor, tells how cages are rattled:

> *It usually happens on the quarterdeck, the open space outside the sleeping and administrative quarters of the drill instructors. It's time to play "fish or cut bait." Time to separate the chaff. All platoons in the training company are gathered and seated on the deck. A folding table is placed on the quarterdeck so that all recruits may see the upcoming proceedings.*
>
> *The series commanding officer, usually a captain, comes in. Recruits are called to attention. The captain takes a seat at the table. To recruits, a captain is higher than God himself. Then the series officers, the lieutenants, and the series first sergeant march in and take their seats. Drill instructors stand in the back of the group. Recruits*

remain at rigid attention. Most have no idea what is about to happen.

One by one, offending recruits—the ones drill instructors feel have no possibility for improvement—are marched in for "office hours." The first sergeant announces the charges. Charges range from willfully disobeying a lawful order to insubordination to a non-commissioned officer.

The captain or the first sergeant reads each recruit his or her rights. Generally, the same basic judicial rights that apply to civilians apply to the military. The recruit can't be forced to testify against him or herself. Double jeopardy is not permitted. Any sentence may be appealed.

Every case is handled separately. The recruit is allowed to testify in his or her defense. The Marine Corps provides the recruit with legal counsel if desired, or the recruit may obtain independent counsel.

The captain may ask questions of the drill instructors, the first sergeant, or the recruit. These questions and their answers provide the captain with the facts to make a judgment.

The captain announces his or her findings. If the recruit is judged guilty, the captain announces punishment. Recruits judged as irrecoverable are normally punished by expulsion from the Corps. Not so often, a recruit is allowed to stay. He or she must convince the court of a sincere desire to change. Be it known that in the upcoming days, any recruit allowed to stay will be watched, monitored, supervised, and controlled. One more incident will send the recruit home.

The memory of commanding officer's office hours stays with the recruits. It has a dramatic effect on those remaining members. Suddenly they realize that the Corps means business. They discover that slackers are not wanted; that laggards will not be tolerated. Morale climbs the charts. The undisciplined are dumped. Only first-rate recruits remain. It's time to get down to the nation's business with men and women of quality.

A Few Good Memories
_____

The mission of the military, especially in the Marine Corps, demands that absolute obedience to a lawful order is essential. Slacking or lagging in combat could be the difference in a battle won and a battle lost, just as the writing of Kipling, who in his poem, explained the consequences of the loss of a nail from a horse's shoe, rings true in the Corps.

Harold J. contributes this following first-hand story to indicate how the DIs turn it up a notch during the second week. This story also shows that in the boot camps of years ago, recruits could be treated with a quite a bit of indecency.

It was the beginning of the second training week of boot camp at Parris Island. The year was 1954. We had drawn our gear, filled out all the forms; and even though we'd been pushed hard, nothing really tough had happened yet. We began to think that this was to be a cakewalk, and that all the horror stories were just propaganda. We had no idea that our DIs were biding their time, letting us dig ourselves in deeper.

In 1954, few restrictions were imposed on DIs as to the punitive treatment of recruits. We were called maggots, dingbats, shitbirds, and a few names I would not want in this book because I expect that maybe my grandchildren will read it one day. In addition to verbal indignities, recruits who couldn't seem to learn at a fast-enough pace could expect to feel the sharp blow of a rifle butt or a DI's combat boot on their backsides.

Our drill instructors enjoyed rousing us for a 0430 reveille. They'd yell and scream and throw GI cans across the squad bay and expel enough air through those whistles in a minute to fill the Hindenburg.

Even so, early morning reveille didn't bother me. I'd lived for eighteen years on a dairy farm in the northwestern part of South Carolina. I was accustomed to rising at 0400 every morning.

A Few Good Memories

One of our junior DIs was especially impolite. He'd pick one recruit each morning and stay on top of him all day. One morning it was my turn to endure him. As I did every morning, I got up early, before reveille, and was already dressed when he entered the squad bay. "Hey, Shitbird," he barked at me. "Why you get up so early?"

I snapped to attention and answered loudly. "Sir. Kind of makes me feel at home. I grew up on a dairy farm. I got up at 0400 every day, sir." I was proud of that fact.

Then I knew I'd said the wrong thing. He turned on me harder than ever before. "OK, Wormshit," he said. "You like 0400, we'll see how you gonna like 0300."

All the next week, the DI on duty racked me out at 0300. I had to clean the heads and get them ready for an 0400 inspection every morning, all of which I failed miserably. I was happy when that week was over.

For weeks afterwards, the question of whether I still appreciated the clock showing 0430 hours was asked of me every morning. By then I'd gotten a lot smarter so I'd always answer, "No, sir" in a most emphatic manner.

9: Adjustments to Military Life

Drill instructors seem to feel a definite attachment to the physical area they rule. Anytime a recruit litters, dirties, or trashes part of the DI's area, it is taken personally. Read this story sent in by Arnie W.

I was a recruit in 1952. Boot camp was tough then. I'm sure every Marine can say that about when he went through, but somehow I have a feeling that mine was the toughest. Do you remember those little square boxes sitting all around the squad bays in a Marine Corps barracks? You know, those little green wooden boxes, a foot square and about six inches high and filled to the brim with pretty, white sand. When a recruit would finish a cigarette, he was supposed to bury the butt in the sand with one end sticking out. These "butt boxes" kept down the possibility of a fire in those old wooden buildings. They also promoted cleanliness. Although regulations required one of these for every twenty men, we could never, ever let our drill instructor, Sgt. Young, catch us using them, and certainly we could not leave a butt sticking out of that sand.

A Few Good Memories

He said that was his *beach, and nobody littered his beach.*

One day, somebody did litter his beach. We were third platoon, B Company. It was a Saturday morning at Parris Island. After two hours on the drill ground, we marched into the "House of Knowledge" to see a training film. Appropriately enough, the title of the film was, "The Late Company B." The story told about a U.S. Army infantry company setting up night defensive positions in France during WWII. The commander had set a fifty percent watch, meaning that at least half of the troops would remain on guard while the others slept.

One by one, the tired U.S. soldiers on watch dropped off to sleep until no one remained on alert. Nazi soldiers overran their positions, killing every American soldier. The NCO in charge of our training class reminded us that every man has absolute responsibilities and he must follow them to the letter, however trivial they may seem. "Had any one of those soldiers been awake, the loss might not have occurred," he said. "Company B was wiped out because men neglected their responsibilities."

At noon we were marched to the chow hall to eat. When we returned to our squad bay, I couldn't believe my eyes. The place was a wreck. Racks were overturned. Mattresses were piled in a corner. Shoes, a dozen or more at a clip, had their laces knotted together. The sand in the butt kits was strewn everywhere. Some recruits had forgotten to lock their footlockers. The contents were mixed in a big heap on the deck.

Sgt. Young, the DI who owned the beaches, came in yelling, "I told you ladies before and I meant it. I do not want my beach littered. Somebody left a butt sticking straight up in my sand. You people messed up my beach. What if the general had come by? You will spend this entire weekend cleaning up this mess. You will go through every one of my butt kits, grain by grain of my sand, and remove every piece of contraband until my sand is as white and pure as it was when I put it in here a year ago."

A Few Good Memories

> "And," he continued, "I will personally inspect my beach when you finish. If I don't approve of how well you cleaned it up, we will start all over."
>
> And, by golly, we did. The DI would inspect. We would fail inspection, so he would re-litter the squad bay. Then he'd re-inspect and we'd fail again. And on and on.
>
> I believe that that lesson was what we needed. Most of us ended up in Korea a few months later. Many of us ended up in the same unit, "E" company of the 2nd battalion, 7th Marine Regiment, 1st Marine Division. Every time watches were assigned, somebody invariably would suggest we not end up like the "Late Company B."

And inspections! Rifle inspections, locker inspections, and bodily health inspections. If an inspection isn't on the schedule, the drill instructor will make up one. Remember junk-on-the-bunk inspections? This inspection requires that recruits lay out all of their clothes and equipment, in an exact, predetermined manner, so that the inspecting officer or NCO may check that each recruit has his or her required issue.

It's not only Parris Island and San Diego where a bit of hazing might be expected. One of the goals of officer training at Quantico is to take the wind from the sails of these soon-to-be new officers.

Robert L. remembers the time he went through OCS at Quantico. He suggested that I entitle this story "Ghost Soldier." So, read Robert's account of the ghost soldier:

> The year was 1964. The Marine Corps shoved more and more officer candidates through Quantico. Vietnam waited in the wings. The barracks building no longer held the usual three platoons. Bunks were added and squeezed in to accommodate five platoons. They must have known that Vietnam would be a long and tough war. The probability of survival for a platoon leader in combat

was counted in days rather than months, and Quantico had to provide for a steady re-supply.

As usual, Saturday was a time of varied inspections. This particular morning, we were ordered to prepare for a junk-on-the-bunk inspection and then parade practice. Our staff platoon leader told us not to empty our laundry bags, just hang them on our rear bedsteads. Otherwise we would look too prepared. The commanding general of Marine Corps Schools, Quantico, would perform the walk-through in what was supposed to be an impromptu visit.

My bunk was topside on the inboard aisle. My "best buddies," Skip and Marvin, had the top and bottom outboard bunks behind me, next to the windows. Our clothing issues were laid out. We worked and slaved until the DI approved every inch of the space. We waited for the general.

Then a commanding "Platoon, Ten Hut!" came booming through the squad bay. We shot to attention. The entourage of majors, colonels, and the general slowly walked down the squad bay aisle, asking hundreds of questions—our service numbers, our rifle numbers, the name of the Marine Corps Commandant, and anything they thought would trip us up. We were sharp. We were prepared.

When they reached my bunk, a major stepped forward and asked me to explain the unusual display of my laundry bag. I remained rigid. My laundry bag was behind me. I would not move without an order.

The major commanded a very military, "About face!" I came about and saw that my half-full laundry bag was balanced, upside down, on the top rail of my bedstead. On the top of the bag sat a perfectly placed service cap, the old "pisscutter," complete with a major's insignia. Had the laundry bag had eyes, a nose, and a mouth, it would have looked exactly like a ghost wearing the cap of a Marine Corps major.

"Well, Candidate!" the major repeated. "Explain this!"

"Sir, I have no idea. I don't know how it got that way."

"Is this your bunk?"

"Yes, sir."

"Who is responsible for your bunk area?"

"I am, sir."

The major turned to our DI and requested that I be trained in the proper procedure for laying out a bunk clothing inspection.

That weekend, I underwent a bunk inspection at 1600 hours and 2000 hours on Saturday, and on Sunday at 0800 hours, 1200 hours, 1600 hours, and 2000 hours. After each inspection, a DI would inspect, then he'd completely tear up the display so that I would have to start over from scratch.

Even though Skip and Marvin denied any part in this setup, I had no doubt that they were responsible. I returned the favor a couple of times.

A Few Good Memories
_____

10: Mail Call

Mail Call stories came in from lots of former and current Marines as well as spouses and significant others. No doubt exists that recruits need and want mail and lots of it. It's their only contact with home. In most cases, immediately after mail call, the Corps allows recruits to have quiet time so the soon-to-be Marines may read their valuable messages from home.

Five times per week, Monday through Friday, and once in a while on Saturday, a drill instructor walks into the recruit squad bay and shouts, "MAIL CALL!" Recruits gather, waiting and hoping for their names to be called. Nothing is more important than a letter from home. Be it from Mom, Uncle Joe, or a very special sweetheart, the words in the letter remove him or her from the "Land that God Forgot," if only for a very few minutes.

This story is from a former Marine, Tom M.:

When we were surviving Marine Corps Boot Camp at San Diego in 1962, privacy was just about non-existent. Our lockers were subject to search and inspection 24/7. So were our footlockers. It was a virtual impossibility to keep anything personal and private, except through the not-so-

A Few Good Memories

very-often good graces of drill instructors. For the most part, the DIs did allow us to have a small amount of privacy, and they let us alone while we read our letters and were mentally transported back home. They rarely bothered a boot's mail either. However, this was true only if it was properly secured in his footlocker.

One hectic day, about half way through our hellish 12 weeks, S/Sgt Towns was on a tear. Most of us had failed our rifle inspection that morning. We were late falling into formation. Nothing seemed to be going right. S/Sgt Towns ordered us to run back into our barracks and saddle up in field marching packs and hard-hats and be back in formation in three minutes.

In trying to accomplish this impossible task, Recruit Smith scurried too quickly. Unknown to Smith, one of his personal letters fell onto the deck and came to rest next to his bunk. The "hawk-eyed" S/Sgt Towns never missed a thing. When the letter fell, it became contraband. No holds were barred. Smith's privacy had flown out of the window.

The platoon did not meet its three-minute deadline. This irritated S/Sgt Towns. He directed us to pack and unpack our field marching packs, over and over again. If the sergeant saw a boot doing a good job, he would walk over to him and scatter the items across the deck.

Finally S/Sgt Towns called the platoon to attention and commanded, "Recruit Smith. Front and center." Smith stepped back out of the ranks, strutted smartly to the front of the platoon, and faced S/Sgt Towns. His back was to us.

"Smith, does a recruit litter his area of the squad bay?"

"Sir, no sir."

"Good, Maggot. We found this letter on the deck in your bunk area. This platoon will identify its source so we may apprehend the guilty party. Do you know anyone who might litter your areas?"

"Sir. No, sir."

"In that case, Recruit, do an about face and read it

to the platoon. Platoon, you will listen up and listen for clues. The offending party must be located."

Smith looked at the letter. His face grew ghostly white. He turned to the DI with a wistful plea written on his face. S/Sgt Towns yelled, "You're wasting my time and the rest of the platoon's time, Maggot! Read!"

Smith's shaky voice read, "My darling baby. It has been so long since you held me in your arms. How much longer will it be?" The platoon burst into riotous laughter. Smith stopped reading.

"Get on with it, Smith," bellowed S/Sgt Towns. Smith continued, his voice cracking intermittently. Smith continued reading how the writer of the letter would love him until the day she died. She revisited very intimate times in their life.

The platoon's laughter soon died. We felt that enough was enough. Smith had received enough ridicule. Who knew the next time it might be one of us. To the best of my knowledge, no one in the platoon ever mentioned that incident again, especially to Smith. From that day forward, every recruit double-checked everybody else's bunk area prior to leaving.

Another story came in, this time from PFC Bryan Post. Bryan is currently serving in the Marine Corps in Hawaii, and he remembers this story well:

Recruit Gregory, the "ladies man" of our San Diego recruit platoon, always got more than his share of mail. He usually had more letters than any of the rest of us—from at least two or three girls every mail call. It became a joke with the rest of us. Maybe we didn't see it as a joke; we were a bit jealous.

One day, just before evening chow, our junior DI called us to attention and bellowed, "Mail call." One by one the recruits' names were called. He would step up, hold his hand out, say, "Thank you, sir," do an about face, and return to his spot in formation.

The DI had not called Gregory's name, and his hand was almost empty. Soon, just six letters remained.

The DI called, "Gregory!"

"Here, sir," he answered and smartly stepped up. "Thank you, sir," and he returned to formation.

Again the DI called, "Gregory!"

Again Gregory stepped up, retrieved his letter, thanked the DI, then returned to his place.

Four more times the DI yelled Gregory's name, he answered, "Here, sir," stepped forward, got his mail, thanked the DI, and returned to formation.

Each time Gregory's name was called, the rest of the platoon would snicker and moan a little louder. The DI would admonish them for grab-assing in ranks.

As Gregory's name was called for the sixth time, the platoon was in stitches. The DI had totally lost control of the platoon, as well as himself. He, too, was laughing—something we had never seen before. A DI laughing? That was something we did not believe could ever happen.

Another mail call story comes from Charles H., who asked that I call the subject recruit Gomer Pyle. Even though it has been many years since this happened, some may remember and may still subject him to verbal abuse:

Every recruit longs for "Mail Call." This is the time when the misery of boot camp is placed into the back of the minds of the recruits and forgotten, if only for a little while. Gomer periodically received mail-order advertisements from Fredericks of Hollywood. Page after page of scantily clad models tried to lure readers into purchasing the clothing items they were wearing. Gomer convinced us that these catalogs were probably ordered for him by someone back home as a joke, but to the DIs, and to us, it didn't matter. The whole platoon, and I'm sure the DIs, anticipated the arrival of the next Fredericks catalog.

A Few Good Memories

As the DI would call out a recruit's name, the recruit would come forward, snap to attention, hold out his arm, and say, "Sir, Recruit so-and-so, sir." The DI would slap the mail into the recruit's hand. The recruit would do an about face and retire to a private location to savor his prizes.

As time went by, the DIs would place all of Recruit Pyle's mail at the bottom of the stack so that he would be last on the list, especially when he had an envelope from Fredericks. Then the fun would begin. Recruit Pyle would have to stand in front of the platoon, holding up this new catalog, and explain to us why each item was invented. He would have to rate the different garments on a scale of one to ten, and tell why he chose each rating.

We believed that the DI stayed up nights thinking of new ways to approach Recruit Pyle when the next Fredericks catalog arrived. Pyle took it well, though, and it became a game. In fact, he became quite adept at the presentations—so adept that we began to call him Recruit Frederick. Even the DIs picked up on it.

The day before graduation, our DI called us all together for one of his last gung-ho meetings. He talked to us about our years ahead, but one of the most moving subjects was when he commended Recruit Pyle for being such a good sport. He asked how many of us would take such a situation and turn it into a positive thing as Pyle had. Few of us could answer in the affirmative. This was a lesson to be learned.

Sally M. is the wife of Max, a retired Marine. It was 1968 and they were sweethearts. They had just graduated from Richland High School in Columbia, South Carolina and were talking about marriage. But with the low-paying jobs available to high school graduates, they knew they could not afford it. They decided that Max would join the Corps instead of being drafted. Sally would live with her parents, go to work in her favorite department store, and save some money for later. Here is Sally's story about mail call:

A Few Good Memories

I missed Max. He was not too far away ... just a little over a hundred miles at Parris Island. But it seemed like a thousand. One day I felt especially melancholy and blue. On one of my work breaks at the department store, I strolled over to the men's department and saw this gorgeous pair of men's undershorts. They were blood red with pictures of yellow tigers all over. I bought them and mailed them to Max.

About ten days later I got this letter from Max asking me not to send anything but letters to him. He told me that the drill instructor saw him open the box and lift out the underwear. For the rest of that day and the all of the following day Max had to wear these shorts over his head!

Mail is wonderful for these soon-to-be warriors. But as any former recruit will tell you, don't get cute. Anything other than a straight, "plain brown wrapper" letter spells trouble. Boot camp is stressful enough in its normal state. Anything beyond that muddies the waters.

A Few Good Memories

11: Physical Conditioning

Any time the word *Marine* is spoken, it invokes the image of a tough, rough-and-ready person who'd accept just about any mission when needed. Listen to television talk shows and game shows. When a Marine appears, some comment is usually made that signifies strength, competency, and uniqueness.

And they are right. But it doesn't come without work. Sure, a recruit must have the innate potential, but his or her body and mind must be *trained* to end up the Marine way.

Physical conditioning is one of the primary means of developing mind and body for the rigors of a Marine's life.

Below is another of Ron M's stories. This one he entitles *Physically Unfit:*

> When I reported to Parris Island in May of 1967, physical readiness was my biggest obstacle. I was a waste. I flunked my first physical fitness test about as miserably as you can imagine. I remember our first run. It was about 0530, just before dawn. We fell in on Panama Street in front of the wooden barracks. Sgt. Bush bellowed, "Right face," then "Dooooooouble, March." We all started running.
>
> For the first five minutes or so, everything seemed fine. I led the pack. Then the pain hit me. First it was

A Few Good Memories

slight, then it grew into an even larger pain. I couldn't seem to draw enough air in my lungs. Then I noticed that I was falling back toward the end of the platoon. After another few minutes I was dead last and still losing ground.

Sgt. Bush evidently had noticed my plight. Before I realized it, he appeared directly behind me. The sergeant's rabbit punch to the small of my back drew an even worse pain. I could still move, but it was extremely painful. He screamed to me that I was in his way. "If you don't move out, Shitface, I'm going to run over you and let them ship your slow butt home in a body bag!"

I had heard of adrenaline, but I had had very little experience with it in civilian life. I found out about it that day. Within five minutes, I was ten feet, then fifteen feet, ahead of the platoon and gaining. The DI's attention switched to another poor soul.

When we returned to our barracks and were dismissed, we entered our squad bay and prepared for our Four S's (Shit, shower, shave, and shampoo). Sgt. Bush came over to me and called the platoon to attention. He told them that, I, Recruit Ron, was obviously the fastest runner in the platoon because I arrived twenty yards ahead of everyone. From now on I would be "hatch body." This meant that I would run with the platoon until I heard the words, "Hatch body out!" I would then speed up and return to the barracks, way ahead of everyone else. I would unlock the hatch to the squad bay, unlock the DI's hatch, and be standing at attention at the entrance when the rest of the platoon arrived.

At first I thought that this would kill me, but actually it was a blessing. I would arrive ahead of everyone and unlock the place. I noticed the DI's scuttlebutt (water cooler). I'd gulp great swallows of the DI's ice water. Boots were only allowed to drink from the regular scuttlebutt. Only DIs could drink ice water. Another advantage was that if I could run fast enough, I would have time to lie in my rack and catch my breath. When I heard Sgt. Bush's big booming voice as they turned *onto the far end of Panama Street, I'd jump up and straighten up my sack. That gave me plenty of time to unlock the DI hatch and run out front to welcome the platoon home. I actually began to look forward to these morning runs.*

Jim T. was an officer candidate at Quantico in 1956. To get those gold bars as a second lieutenant meant you must be in no less the physical condition as the men or women you will later command. As in boot camp at Parris Island and San Diego, the lack of physical fitness will fail a candidate.

Read Jim's story. He asked that a fictitious name be used, so again we'll sacrifice Gomer Pyle.

One of the events at the officer candidate training area's obstacle course at Quantico was nothing more than a series of 2x4 frames built over a four-foot deep lake. It wasn't really a lake, but a trough of slimy, filthy water about fifteen feet wide. We called it "The Pit." The staff kept the muck and mire well mixed by dragging the bottom with a hoe-like contraption just before we began our pit exercises. To fall into the channel meant extra hours of rifle, equipment, and uniform cleaning. Some officer candidates would throw away their utilities and buy another set.

The object of this course was to cross ladders hand-over-hand, swing from ropes, and make your way across the fifty-yard long course, without falling. Pyle was rotund and short. He came from a classy family in upper New York State. He'd probably never climbed anything in his life except the social ladder.

One day at about 1600 hours our platoon was marched to The Pit. We had not slept for over 30 hours because of a night exercise the evening before. We were dragging, to say the least.

A Few Good Memories

Half the platoon had completed the obstacle course the first time. Then Pyle started his run. He managed the first ladder and then grabbed the rope and put everything he had into it when he shoved off, trying to cross the fifteen-foot-wide chasm and land on the safety of the 8x8 girder. Only he didn't have enough power in his leap. He swung short of the crossbeam by about three or four inches.

Still hanging onto the rope, he swung back in the direction he had come from, only not as far. Then he swung back in the opposite direction. Back and forth he oscillated, finally coming to a dead stop directly over The Pit. Pyle yelled for help. The DI told him to find a way. "Do it yourself, Pyle. I won't be with you when you're fighting your way in to the beach."

His hands held on to the rope as long as they could. Every couple of seconds his grip failed slightly and he dropped another inch or two down the rope.

Every DI joined in. They had no mercy. They shouted and taunted with orders to get on with the course. Everyone else had finished and Pyle was still hanging over the muck and mire. We couldn't believe how long he hung on.

Finally he dropped straight down. Pyle and his rifle disappeared under the gooey, dirty mess. He stood up and started crawling, slowly making his way toward the edge. Two more times he slipped and went under. Finally, he climbed out and just stood there, looking no less horrible than the Creature from the Black Lagoon.

Pyle soaked as long as they'd let him in the showers after we were dismissed. For the next week he failed every rifle inspection because of a dirty rifle. The poor guy tried, but we all know that a DI can find dirt in and on a rifle, come hell or high water.

Pyle was dropped from the officer program a couple of weeks later. As far as we could tell, this incident was not the sole reason. Many other transgressions added

A Few Good Memories

up to lack of fitness to be a Marine officer. But this incident at The Pit obviously took its toll.

Mole crickets and sand fleas thrive at Parris Island. But don't hurt any of these animals because who knows to whom they belong.

This is Jerry R's story:

The sun was hot and the humidity unbearable at Parris Island during that summer of 1972. I kept wondering why the hell I'd joined the Corps. We were on one of S/Sgt Brown's "afternoon strolls." He had a way with words. As we covered mile after mile at a fast trot, every inch of my body was slippery wet. Every thread sloughed off unabsorbed sweat.

I, like some of the rest of my platoon, was not too cooperative that day. The sergeant stayed on my butt. Every time I'd put out less than a hundred percent effort, he'd raise hell.

Finally, S/Sgt Brown gave the signal: "All right, Maggots. Crap Out. Ten minutes." I fell in my tracks. About that time, this stupid looking little mole cricket crawled by. I was in a bad mood. Deep inside me, I guess, I had to relieve my tension. The mole presented an opportunity. I sneered at the little prehistoric-looking creature. I thought about how lucky he was to be free to go about as he pleased, and if he pleased. So I whacked him hard with my hand, and smashed him to a pulpy mess.

Then I heard Brown. "What was that?" He knew what was that. He must have been looking dead at me when I smashed it. He walked over and looked at the now-deceased mole cricket. He picked it up and stared into my eyes.

"Look, Maggot. See this? You just killed the lieutenant's pet cricket. Why? Answer up. Now!" A maggot is not allowed lie. A maggot is not allowed to be

sorry. A maggot must take responsibility for his sins. Finally, a maggot must offer payback for his wayward ways. Only, this time the whole platoon had to join in.

We spent two hours scratching and digging in the sand, looking for a replacement for the lieutenant's pet mole cricket. "If we don't find one," Brown reminded us over and over, "the lieutenant is going to get damn well hacked off. And you know what happens when the lieutenant gets hacked off. He jumps on my ass. Then I get hacked off. And you know what happens when I get hacked off. I jump on your ass. Is that what you want, Ladies?"

"No, Sir!" (in unison).

Oh, we found plenty of mole crickets. Some were too large. Others were too small. Some had grins on their faces. Others had frowns. One was missing a leg and the lieutenant would not stand for a disabled mole cricket.

Finally, somebody found a perfect mole cricket. It was turned over to me to guard, love, care for, and transport back to the barracks, under threat of death if it didn't make it. I took out one of my spare socks and wrapped it up and placed it gently in my pocket.

We came back to our area at 1730 and lined up for mess call—all sixty recruits and one mole cricket. SSgt. Brown told me that the lieutenant would see me at 0700 sharp the next morning. At that time I would present him with the healthy mole cricket. I struggled to keep the cricket alive that night. I figured that at 0700 all my worries would be over.

Brown had me at the lieutenant's hatch at 0655. At 0700 I knocked three times. "Enter!" boomed the voice of God, alias the lieutenant. I opened the hatch and strutted forward. I stood at rigid attention and requested to speak to the lieutenant. "Speak, Recruit," he bellowed.

"Sir, I have a replacement for your pet mole cricket." That brought all sorts of questions concerning very exhaustive details of where was his other mole cricket and why he had to get another mole cricket. No explanation seemed to be adequate.

A Few Good Memories

> "Let's see it," he said. I handed it to him. He stared at the little creature. His eyes covered the cricket from top to bottom. He looked at it from the front, from the rear. A frown grew on his face. "This is a stupid-looking cricket," he growled as he dropped the cricket onto the deck and smashed it under his boot heel.

This story from William H. is obviously a lesson by his drill instructor to teach a platoon of recruits the difference between port and starboard. To be a real Marine, one must know the difference between port and starboard. Whether you are a recruit or a general officer, there is neither left nor right; it is either port or starboard. Few unindoctrinated civilians know the meaning of the words. Therefore, drill instructors must take great pains in teaching boots the difference.

> *In the middle seventies, I was putting up with the early training days at Parris Island. One day, our DI told us that each of us would some day see duty aboard a U.S. Naval vessel. We must learn the difference between port and starboard. The DI's cardinal approach to teaching port and starboard was to use our mattresses from our bunks. We would stand this drill in our squad bay.*
>
> *We first were ordered to take our mattress pads off our bunks and stand at attention in the center aisle. We'd start with the mattress pad at our starboard (right) side. At the order, "Port side," we were to hoist our cumbersome mattress pads and move them over to our port (left) sides. Then the DI would command, "Starboard side." We would then pick up the mattress pads and move them over to our right sides.*
>
> *This went well for quite a while. The DI alternated from port to starboard to port, etc, each time. But he soon began calling orders in random sequence, such as "Port side," then "Starboard side," then sometimes he'd repeat "Starboard side." Sometimes the same command would be*

repeated four of five times in a row, trying to catch us off guard.

At the command, "Maggots, Attention," we would immediately put down our mattress pads and stand square. All recruits on the wrong side of their racks were given ten, twenty, or more pushups.

After nearly an hour we got the hang of it. The DI had trouble getting any more pushups. Never to be outsmarted, the DI commanded, "Port side," then "Attention." We all stood at attention on what should have been the correct side of our mattress pad. The artful DI looked us over and yelled, "You idiots, the ship is headed in the opposite direction. Every one of you dumbirds got your bunk pad on the wrong side. Now everybody get down! Gimme twenty!"

12: Cleanliness

Remember how clean everything stayed at Boot Camp? It was not by accident. When everything seemed to be caught up, something dirty could always be found. And if a DI couldn't find something dirty, he'd find something else to do.

William H. remembers:

Seven days a week we cleaned and swabbed and polished. We longed for a free day, an afternoon, an hour, or just a free minute or two. But we learned not to count on it. The training schedules listed free time as the thirty-minute period before taps. That was a laugh.

Back home, civilian kids our ages were outside playing football or baseball, or making a little time with their favorite girl friends. Not us. We were stuck with heads to swab, brass to polish, or that eternally dirty M-1 rifle to clean. Our DI would always remind us, "Some day you maggots will live or die by the condition of your equipment."

A Few Good Memories

>   *It was April 1961, at San Diego on a Sunday afternoon. As usual, all sixty of us recruits lay sprawled over the squad bay deck rubbing polish on the rifle stocks, neatsfoot oil on the sling, or shoving rifle patches down the rifle barrels with cleaning rods.*
>
>   *The Quonset hut ports (windows) were open to allow the warming spring breezes to drift through. Lots of griping and bitching was in progress. Our DI always told us that bitching recruits were happy recruits, so we must have been the happiest recruits on earth.*
>
>   *Suddenly a bird, a large bird, flew into the squad bay through one of the ports. He started flopping against the bulkheads (walls). He couldn't find his way out. We were positive he'd hurt himself. Someone yelled to the DI, "Sir, there's a bird in the squad bay, Sir."*
>
>   *Very calmly, without a second of hesitation, the DI fired back. "We don't have time to mess with that stupid bird now. Get back to cleaning those rifles. You got rifle inspection in twenty minutes. The maggot with the cleanest rifle can take Tweety out and kill his ass."*

Cleaning heads, decks, bulkheads, etc., is a chore that Marines get used to doing. The secret to getting these distasteful chores done with a minimum of hassle is to keep a happy outlook. But not too happy.

This story comes from Robert W. about a fellow member of his platoon in Boot Camp:

>   *It was 1954 and I was at Parris Island. Every time we turned around, the DIs blamed us for dirty heads (bathrooms). It had to be just hassle because we scrubbed them till our knuckles were raw. When he would jump on us, most of us would groan, but certainly under our breath, and never where the DI could see.*
>
>   *We couldn't figure out one of the recruits in our platoon. He was from Dundalk, Maryland, and was a good*

A Few Good Memories

guy, but for one thing. He was always smiling. He couldn't keep the smile off his face. It was bad enough when the DIs chewed out other recruits, but he smiled even more when he was the object of discipline. We named him "Laughing Boy." He laughed about that, too.

One day our JDI (junior DI) had just about had enough. We were exhausted, but still proudly marching in from a full-pack forced march. The DI yelled every step of the way and, sure enough, Laughing Boy had a foot-wide grin on his face.

"Platoon, halt," the JDI commanded. We were ordered to fall out and form a semi-circle around Laughing Boy. We were told that it was our mission to find some way to stop that recruit's stupid smiling or the whole platoon would suffer.

"Corporal, Sir. I think I know a way," said this six-foot, three-inch beanpole recruit from a small town in western Tennessee.

"OK, Wadkins. You try. I give up. But if you can't make it work, this whole platoon will run two miles every day after evening chow, until the maggot learns to quit smiling."

Wadkins stood in front of the five-foot, ten-inch Laughing Boy. He made the young recruit look like a midget. We waited for the huge Tennessean to start pounding the recruit into the ground. He didn't. He spoke in a calm, reserved manner. "Laughing Boy, I used to laugh when my mama would fuss at me back home in the hills. I was mean. She was a good woman and I didn't treat her right."

The DI seemed to get impatient. "Get on with it, Wadkins. We ain't got all day."

"Yes, Sir." Wadkins turned back to Laughing Boy. "Take your hand and pull that grin off your ugly face, Laughing Boy. Then sling it down to the deck. Real hard."

He did. "Now stomp on it! Kill it!"

Laughing Boy stomped and stomped. He still had the grin spread ten inches across his face.

A Few Good Memories

  The DI saw what was happening and pitched in, "Take your bayonet and stab it to death, Maggot." Laughing Boy stabbed and stomped until he must've been exhausted. He still had the grin.

  The DI soon ordered the rest of the platoon to stomp and stab. After a good ten minutes, the DI proclaimed the grin dead. A burial service was called to order. Laughing Boy dug a deep hole with his entrenching tool while the rest of his squad collected some palmetto leaves and formed a makeshift coffin around the deceased grin. For some reason it worked. The grin disappeared, even when the DI yelled and screamed at him. Each member of the platoon participated in shoveling the dirt back into the hole.

  The platoon was called to attention and Laughing Boy was directed to sing the Marine Corps Hymn, then Amazing Grace. He knew the words to the Marine Hymn, but we couldn't recognize the music part; and he had a great deal of difficulty piecing together enough words to Amazing Grace. The burial site was marked with two small sticks tied together to form a cross.

  From then on, every time our platoon passed the gravesite of the grin, we'd stop for a moment and bow our heads in reverence. Laughing Boy would say a prayer. The last week of our training was devoted to preparing for graduation. On Wednesday, the DIs marched us to the gravesite of the grin. The JDI pulled up the cross and handed it to Laughing Boy. I would bet that he still has it today among his souvenirs.

A Few Good Memories

13: Gotchas

Pranks are common in the field once boot camp is over. They are usually pulled on new Marines and sometimes have dramatic results.

One common and interesting prank that I ran into while flying in the Marine Corps was for a maintenance NCO to grab a new man and send him to another squadron with a bucket and ask to borrow five gallons of "prop wash." Marines who have been around for more than a week know that prop wash is the flow of air from an aircraft's propeller as it spirals toward the rear in a gale-like gust.

South Carolina is located on the Southeastern Coast of the United States, precisely in the path of a lot of hurricanes that come up from the warm waters of the Caribbean Sea. The mere mention of a hurricane sends chills through people who understand their consequences.

Boot camp is usually not a place for pranks, but Michael M. tells this story of a prank that did happen in boot camp:

A Few Good Memories

It was February 1960, and the outside air at Parris Island was very chilly, even to a recruit from the great state of South Dakota. Our drill instructor had been quite easy on us for a couple of days. Somebody said it was the calm before the storm.

One morning at first formation, our DI told us that a hurricane had been sighted off the coast of South Carolina and it was headed our way. To protect the property of the United States Marine Corps, it would be our job to move all of our footlockers out of our squad bay over to the "Sand Box." The Box was a thirty-yard-long trench of fine beach sand about ten feet wide and dug into the ground ten feet deep. In the Box, we would continue our training, being protected from the violent winds from the hurricane when it arrived.

After morning chow, the DI put us in formation again and explained that it was time; we must take our footlockers and our bunks immediately to the Box and set up for three or four days of inconvenience. The hurricane was almost here. We had ten minutes to complete the move. We did it, but it took about fifteen minutes.

We started morning training. Most of us kept staring at the sky for some sign of bad weather. The sun was bright. The sky was clear. At noon chow, we noticed that none of the other platoons had moved. In fact, everybody seemed to be going about the day's business without concern. Then we headed for "the range," a dirty and grimy field filled with briars, for our scheduled hand-to-hand combat training.

We arrived back at the Box at 1700. Our DI told us that the hurricane had fizzled, and that we were to move back into our squad bay in time for evening chow. Since we were scheduled for chow at 1730 hours; that left very little time for the whole platoon to move and for us to hit the showers. But we did it.

After chow, the DI made an inspection of the squad bay, finding millions of grains of fine, white sand on the floor (deck), on our footlockers, our bunks, and all points in between. We finished janitorial work (known to Marines as a field day) at taps (2200 hours).

The next morning at first formation, the DI announced that we must be a stupid bunch of maggots. "Don't you idiots know that hurricane season is from June through November? And don't you know that when a hurricane is coming, the whole sky gets cloudy, the wind blows, and the rain gets heavy? Remind me never to go into combat with you jerks."

Rod C. is a former Marine. He said that his junior drill instructor was hell on wheels. Listen to his story:

We had a lot of parades while I was a boot at Parris Island in 1957. On one particular Saturday morning, our junior drill instructor had been giving me a lot of grief. I had fallen out twenty seconds late that morning and I couldn't convince him that my shoe came off while I was running to formation. Now I was suffering for it.

"You, Recruit, get over here," he yelled at me as we waited for the parade to start. A 105mm howitzer sat at the end of the field. It had a gun crew who fired blanks from it at appropriate times during the ceremonies.

"Take this bucket and run over to the howitzer crew and get this bucket full of muzzle velocity. And get back, on the double. Move it!"

I ran with all my heart and saluted the corporal and asked him for a full bucket of muzzle velocity. He ordered me about face, and in a few seconds, handed me the bucket. I high-tailed it back to my platoon and handed the bucket to the DI.

"Maggot," he yelled. "You spilled half of it. Get back over to that howitzer crew and this time get a full bucket. What can I do with a half a bucket of muzzle velocity? And get back in a hurry. This parade is about ready to start."

A Few Good Memories

> *Off I went, this time running even faster. I saluted the corporal again and told him I'd spilled some of it and needed a full bucket. He took the bucket, about faced me, and handed the bucket back to me.*
>
> *I hurried back to my platoon and handed the bucket to the sergeant. He went into orbit. "Can't you do anything right? What's going to happen in combat when you do your platoon leader like you're doing me? You don't have a third of a bucket left."*
>
> *Next, he gave me two buckets and told me that our supply was really getting low. "Fill up these and move your ass. I see the colonel getting up on the platform. Now, go!"*
>
> *When I got back with those two buckets, he told me that I'd brought back the wrong stuff. "We want 50-caliber muzzle velocity," he yelled. He needed 50-caliber muzzle velocity and I brought back recoil. "Where in the hell do recruiters find you guys," he groaned.*

William H. contributed a couple of stories for this book. Here is one about mountain climbing:

> *Few of us recruits went to Parris Island thinking that we might have an opportunity to do some mountain climbing while we were there. But, leave it to some ingenious DI to invent a new way to create havoc within a platoon of recruits.*
>
> *We thought that since only three days remained until graduation, we had about had all of the jostling we'd have. I think we started to get a little salty. So our DI, S/Sgt. Bowen, saw that it was time to turn up the heat in order to cool us down.*
>
> *"Fall in for mountain climbing drill," he yelled. "Three ranks." We fell in formation in the middle of our squad bay. We never heard of mountain climbing drill, but what the hell—only three more days.*

A Few Good Memories

It turned out that mountain climbing, DI style, meant getting on all fours (hands and feet—no knees) and "climbing" up and down the squad bay. In other words, walking on hands and feet. DI-style mountain climbing is not done at a leisurely pace. It is done as fast as the DI commands.

Rest periods are also not allowed in DI-style mountain climbing. In fact, the longer we climbed, the faster we were ordered to ascend. The sounds of high-top shoes hitting the concrete drowned out just about everything else.

Shortly, S/Sgt. Bowen told us to continue climbing; he had to check in at this office next door. "Remember, I can hear you," he said as he left.

Some smart guy in the platoon came up with the idea that we could just stomp loudly with our shoes while the DI was gone. One recruit was assigned as a DI lookout and was stationed at the door (known to Marines as a hatch). This mountain climbing was fun, especially when we knew we were shoving it down the DI's throat.

Our DI lookout watched. We stomped. Some of us even sat down on the footlockers and slammed our shoes to the deck. You've never seen such a cocky group. We were proud of ourselves.

They say all good things come to an end. DIs always seemed to have a sixth sense about what was going on. S/Sgt. Bowen did. We should have posted two DI lookouts. Suddenly the rear hatch opened and there stood Sgt. Brown in all his glory, smiling, hands on hips.

We finished climbing those mountains at 0200 the next morning. Needless to say that S/Sgt. Bowen's extended mountain climbing session did us little good during the lengthy graduation parade practice the next day.

14: Mess Duty

All recruits serve on mess duty, but certainly not until they've been in training for a while. New recruits haven't learned enough about military discipline to be turned loose immediately. They come into the Corps as "the master of their lives," having had little idea of what "following the rules" means. It's one thing for a recruit to goof up during close-order drill, to make up a rack as if still back in Boise, or to fall out for inspection with a dirty rifle. These errors may be easily overcome with practice and a lot of attention from the DI. However, when it comes to mess hall performance, goofing up swings a wide swath. Marines have to have good chow, not the kind that brand new recruits might produce.

Recruits will take their turns at mess duty after four to five weeks of learning and absorbing strict regulations and learning the ropes. Mess duty does offer a small opportunity for recruits to get away with a little devilment sometimes. And as we all know, devilment is done mostly for the thrill, not for the end results.

A Few Good Memories

Read this story from Larry W.:

Mess duty was a kind of a relief for us recruits, even though we had to get up at 0230. I was pulling my turn at mess duty at Parris Island boot camp in 1965. Our barracks was next door to the mess hall.

One particular day, the menu called for cherry pies for evening mess. The mess sergeant pointed at me, along with two other recruits, and assigned us to cook these pies. He gave us the precise cooking instructions, including the exact number of cans of cherries, the pounds of flour, pound of sugar, etc. This was going to be fun. I'd never cooked before.

With three shaved heads together, hidden from the mess sergeant, we plotted to make an extra pie, one, just for us. Who'd count? We might be able to sneak it over to the barracks next door and eat it during our mid-afternoon rest break.

It worked, except that instead of just one pie, we made three extra pies; a pie for each of us. It was tough keeping them hidden, but we did; and at 1400 hours we covered our crime by sneaking the pies out of the cooking containers. As we left, we hid the pies by wrapping them in our mess shirts. We ran to the empty barracks building and sat down to eat.

Were they good? Were they! As we ate, we realized that we could not leave a trace. We had to eat every scrap of every pie so we wouldn't leave any clues. We couldn't throw uneaten pie into the GI can (trash can). That would be a dead giveaway. So we just kept eating.

By 1430, every ounce of the evidence had disappeared into our stomachs. We had forced ourselves to eat every last morsel of those pies. Then I started to feel a little woozy. So did my two partners in crime. It was almost 1500, time to report back to the mess hall for evening chow duty, when I found that I was too sick to move. So were my accomplices. However, we knew we absolutely had to show up for work.

A Few Good Memories

It was tough, miserable duty that afternoon. The final result of the great pie-eating caper was the lesson we learned. We chose to eat the whole pies, but we still had our responsibilities to fulfill afterwards.

Sometimes recruits get tired, even when on mess duty. Read what Bryan Post saw at San Diego.

Recruits are not allowed to lean. They mustn't lean on a pole, against a tree, or anything, no matter how tired they are. As our platoon waited to go inside the "House of Knowledge" for a class, our DI, Sgt. Williams, used this waiting time to teach us a new drill move. We would be learning that new move the next day during drill practice.

Sgt. Williams was deeply involved in teaching when all of a second he stopped talking, charged off like a gazelle, and bolted over some shrubbery. He hit the ground running and then we saw why. There, behind a storage shed, a recruit in his mess duty uniform was leaning against the side of the building. It appeared that he was hiding. Sgt. Williams arrived on the scene and began chewing on this recruit like I'd never seen. They were only twenty or so yards away so we could hear every word. (Right then and there I made up my mind I'd never lean against anything.)

You'd have thought that leaning against a wall was just short of treason. Sgt. Williams kept chewing. The recruit stood at rigid attention. Finally, the mess sergeant appeared and helped Sgt. Williams chew on the recruit. Then the mess sergeant called for one of his NCOs to go into the mess hall and call out the other recruits from his platoon who were on mess duty.

We continued to watch. The recruits were told that they were in the middle of a crisis. Their stupid fellow recruit had leaned against the wall so long that the shed was in danger of toppling over. Now everybody must go to the opposite side of the building and try to straighten up the shed. They pushed. They grunted. They shoved.

The DI and the mess sergeant continued to run around and yell and berate and scream at first one recruit, then another. Finally, Sgt. Williams and the other DIs pronounced the building safe and back to its original state.

Sgt. Williams raced back to where we remained in formation. Just as if he had never left, he picked up on his instruction with almost the exact word that he was speaking when he left us.

A Few Good Memories
───────────────

15: Close-Order Drill

In the military services, officers and NCOs train their troops to follow orders in almost a "blind obedience" fashion. Imagine the chaos on the battlefield if troops were allowed to decide for themselves which commands to obey and which to ignore. When a platoon leader instructs one of his squads to "hold our left flank," the leader must know that he can trust his squad to do as they were told to the best of their ability. The squad leader might not know at the moment why he must hold the flank, but he must understand that holding the left flank could be critical to the success of the battle.

Obedience at this level is achieved by different training regimens. Among these forms of training is close-order drill. Troops learn to follow close-order drill commands in almost subliminal fashion. They learn to follow commands instantly and without question. A well-trained troop unit on the drill field will look as if one person is drilling in front of 60 well-positioned mirrors.

George W., a former Marine, sent in this story. It's not a humorous one. It's not even a story from boot camp. But it is one that explains the mindset of a lot of Marines. After reading this story, few questions should remain as to why the Marine Corps is one of the finest and most successful fighting organizations in the world.

Back in the late fifties, the company gunnery sergeant in my unit at Camp Lejuene included a very gung-ho GySgt Long. I remember him as a very dedicated Marine who would follow every command to the very best of his superior abilities. He hated any Marine who slacked off and failed to give at least one hundred percent effort.

GySgt Long was unmarried. He often said that if the Corps had wanted him to have a wife, they would have issued him one. He never wore civilian clothes on liberty. He said that, while on liberty, his uniform kept him reminded that he was a Marine and that he must hold fast to superior conduct.

Gunny Long told me one Monday that he had gone on liberty on Sunday and the civilians were disgusting. "They don't do nothing but mill around and ain't a damn soul in charge," he said.

Gunny believed that close-order drill is what got recruits in shape at boot camp. From this they learned discipline. He implemented a company procedure in his unit at Camp Lejeune whereby any Marines restricted for the weekend would fall out at certain times on Saturday and Sunday and engage in close-order drill. Any corporal who fell into the restricted category would be in charge of commanding the drill sessions. Two things happened during the time the gunny's orders remained in effect: The number of Marines sentenced to restriction fell dramatically; and, the troops relearned the finer aspects of close-order drill.

The gunny's strategy certainly worked. He knew that close-order drill builds teamwork and an obedient spirit. He also knew that Marines, like most other humans, actually want to do a good job. Sometimes they must be reminded. The gunny was good at that.

A Few Good Memories

Sometimes lessons are learned not when sitting in a training class, but in a way and a time that we least expect.

Mike S. went through Marine Boot Camp at San Diego Recruit Training Depot in 1977. This is his story about learning military discipline:

>Our drill instructors thought that close-order drill was so important to the mindset and discipline of future Marines that they initiated a drill competition among platoons. Competition would take place once in a while during regular drill practices. Usually two to three platoons would compete. The most junior DI would have control of each platoon. Platoons with fewer than a couple of weeks training would not be ready yet. Since competition wasn't a sanctioned event, the winning platoon would enjoy the knowledge that they had won, but nothing else.
>
>This was 1977 and before the Marines came up with their new battle helmets. We wore the old steel helmet with a plastic liner. For these drill competitions we would wear our liners without the steel helmet.
>
>The breezes coming in from the ocean in San Diego got pretty strong on some days. Sometimes the wind was so intense it was hard to stand up straight. Very often a couple of recruits would have their liners blow off their heads while we were drilling. The DIs would give us a fit about keeping our liners on.
>
>The word got around that the DIs were letting us compete, so one day the series commander (a captain) and the series officers (our lieutenants) came out to watch. The DIs asked the officers to judge the winner.
>
>The wind was especially strong that day. Each platoon drilled at the same time, as the captain and the lieutenants watched and took notes. Helmet liners started to hit the deck as the wind blew them off the recruits' heads. Some recruits would bend over and grab these liners and continue marching.

A Few Good Memories

Two recruits in our platoon lost their liners at the same time but continued to march as if nothing had happened. Those liners sat in the middle of the drill field until the end. I thought we were going to get chewed out because we let our liners fall off.

I was wrong. I learned a lot that day. We won the competition. The captain came over and congratulated us. He told us that we did the right thing to continue marching when our helmets hit the deck. That was why we won. I learned a lot that day about military discipline.

Close-order drill is the root of military discipline. Older Marines say that you may judge the morale and discipline of a unit if you watch them on the drill field or in a parade. Maybe this is why, when you see a Marine unit in a Fourth of July parade, it stands head and shoulders above any other portion of the parade.

16: Combat Pool

The very mission of the Corps demands Marines to be excellent swimmers. At any given time, at least a third of us are on the sea. The Corps developed amphibious landing techniques. The Corps has used these techniques well. Remember WWII in the Pacific—Guadalcanal, Peleliu, Tarawa. Then in Korea, the Marine Corps scored a huge victory with their landing at Inchon. This unexpected and successful landing sent the North Koreans on the run back toward the North.

In boot camp, recruits go through a stage called Combat Water Survival. It is possible for a new recruit to enter through the Red Gate as a non-swimmer. It is not possible, however, for a Marine to depart the Big Red Gate as a non-swimmer.

This Combat Water Survival course is not designed for recruits to pass a little time playing around in the water. No swimsuits are allowed here. Water training is done in fighting gear; camouflage uniforms.

Recruits have an opportunity to achieve different levels of proficiency. The minimum is termed CWS-4, which means that a recruit rated as a "level 4" has demonstrated water survival and life-saving proficiency necessary to perform any standard Marine Corps mission. Ambitious recruits may earn even higher ratings, all the way up to a CWS-1. These higher ratings are earned by

A Few Good Memories

swimming greater distances, longer durations of flotation, and a heavier load of combat gear, including rifles, knives, and pack.

When recruits enter the combat pool area each day, they are given an opportunity for a quick head (restroom) break. The staff isn't too restrictive about recruits taking a few seconds longer than normal. The alternative could be disastrous.

It was disastrous for Henry L., back in 1965 at Parris Island.

> *I was a good swimmer and wasn't concerned about completing water training. I thought I might be able to earn at least a CWS-2.*
>
> *Back then, the pool staff was pretty tough on recruits and not too lenient about the amount of time we could stay in the head. Before we could get in the pool, fifty-seven male recruits had to try to rid their bodies of their excess liquid waste at the urinal. One day, two recruits (I was one) required the use of the commode. The other recruit beat me to the stall, forcing "poor me" to have to wait.*
>
> *The DIs started yelling for all recruits to assemble in the pool stands. The result was that I didn't get my turn at the commode. I was in a world of hurt. If I had been smart, I would have explained my predicament to the DI, but fear kept me silent.*
>
> *About fifteen minutes after my section was ordered into the water, my bodily functions switched to automatic. One of the members of the pool staff detected the foreign waste material coming from me and going in the water. They cleared the pool.*
>
> *They had to drain the pool that day. And naturally I was "volunteered" by the pool staff to be one of the recruits to spend all of my spare time scrubbing. In fact I even scrubbed the walkways outside of the pool area. I got*

plenty of harassment from that. Plus the DI named me "shitbird," which hung in there until graduation.

One thing is for sure. Recruits should remain as inconspicuous as possible. Remember from a previous chapter: (1) shoot the shit, (2) get a receipt, and (3) move with the largest group.

This story is from Clarence J.:

Floating around the Marine Corps are hundreds of informal and certainly unofficial creeds and doctrines to which Marines must adhere or surely suffer the consequences. One of these "guides for living" is that Marines do not sing or hum unless their enlistment papers specify that they are to serve in the band.

Ted, one of the boots in our recruit platoon at San Diego, was always humming, whistling, or singing little tunes to himself. We could never decode his sounds and mostly he did this when the DI's were not present. Once when we were in Pool Week, Ted goofed up and started humming a little tune too audibly during a ten-minute rest period during swim week.

One of the DIs at the pool was Corporal Gray. He seemed to enjoy his work of making life miserable for us recruits. We all felt he was either trying to impress the senior NCOs or that he had a hate for life. We just knew he had a desire to drown all of us.

Corporal Gray's ears picked up the humming sound and quickly located its source. He called the platoon to attention and summoned Ted front and center. Gray asked Ted lots of questions, such as were you a choirboy in civilian life, or did you ever sing opera, or does your mama think you're a singer.

Ted became terribly frustrated and babbled all of his answers. Gray poured it on faster and heavier. Finally, Gray gave the command to Ted, "About face,"

A Few Good Memories

which put Ted facing the platoon.

The DI then commanded us to fall out, and had us sit on the deck with our eyes on Ted.

"Now, Maggot," Gray directed. "Let's get this singing stuff out of your system. Entertain us. As a start, you will sing every verse of the Marine Corps Hymn."

Ted just stood there. I can still remember that pitiful expression on his face.

"Sir, I can't, sir."

"You can't? What do you mean you can't? You telling me you didn't memorize all the verses? You do want to be a Marine don't you?"

"Sir, yes sir."

"Then start singing. Now!"

He started:

"From the halls of Montezuma, to the shores of Tripoli. We fight our country's battles, in the air, on land, and sea. ..."

Ted stopped.

"Get on with it, Boot."

"I forgot the rest."

That did it. Boots must learn every stanza, every verse, every word of the Hymn during the first week of boot camp. A boot must know this from memory.

Gray then relaxed his grip on the poor guy just a bit. He called the platoon to attention and lined us up in a column of threes facing the pool. He had Ted lead us in the singing of the Hymn. Every time we sang a line, the next three recruits in the columns were supposed to jump in the pool, then swim to the sides, climb out, and run get in line again. All this time Ted was ordered to keep singing the Marine Corps Hymn.

Finally the DI stopped us and told Ted that the next time he heard any singing or humming in the platoon, he would not let us off so easy. To his dismay, we nicknamed poor Ted "Choirboy" after that. And the only music heard around the depot after that came from the San Diego Recruit Depot Marine Band.

A Few Good Memories

MSgt Tracy B. became a Marine at Parris Island in autumn of 1977. While at boot camp Tracy and her fellow recruits noticed that every day at 1300, a far-off factory whistle blasted the air with a series of short blasts over a period of one minute. This her story:

Several times during the day, the DIs would order all of us recruits to start singing. By having us sing, they knew where each one of us was at any moment. One girl in the platoon, Cheryl, was blessed with a very pretty country-music-style voice. Sometimes she would be ordered to sing solo. She'd usually sing a sad, sad song, such as "Choctaw Ridge." This would bring tears from our eyes because we were lonely and homesick, and we remembered families back home.

One day during swim week we were standing by, waiting while the DIs screamed at the last couple of stragglers to join us before beginning our next activity. Our DI spotted a friend and walked over to see her. But first she ordered us to sing "I've Been Working on the Railroad" until she returned. Just about the time we reached the "Dinah won'tcha blow your horn," the factory whistle cracked the air. At first, this coincidence was merely humorous. With each additional short burst of the whistle, it seemed that we were back on "Dinah won'tcha blow your horn." We started chuckling. Chuckles turned into laughter and soon we were rolling.

Three DIs, including our own DI, heard the commotion and leapt out of the hut and took control. Even all of the pushups and mountain climbers we did the rest of the afternoon couldn't stop us from laughing.

That night, after lights out, it didn't take very long for everyone to drift off to sleep. Except for the Cheryl, that is. When all was quiet, she boomed out with, "Dinah won'tcha blow your horn." The squad bay came alive with laughter, which brought out the DIs, a march to the parade ground, and a long session of physical training in the dark of the night!

A Few Good Memories

17: Movement Under Fire

What is the real mission of the Marine Corps? Ask any Marine and he'll tell you that his job is to kick anybody's ass any time they get in the way of this country's commitments and principles. That's a wide definition, but it ties neatly into a bundle and makes it easy to understand for all concerned. Whether it's enlisted training at Parris Island and San Diego, or officer training at Quantico, every Marine learns the basics of fighting. They all learn it the same way—the Marine Corps way.

A former Marine sent an email in which he stated that there is only one end result of Marine Corps combat. That one result is to *win*. The only alternative in combat is to win—to win big and with finality. Chesty Puller said it right in one of his writings. Paraphrased, he said that the only way we can be sure that an enemy soldier won't engage us again is to kill him.

We don't need any more halfway actions of the past, like Korea, Vietnam, and the little costly battles, such as Bosnia and Somalia. Even Desert Storm pulled up a bit short. Now the War on Terrorism seems to be on the right track. One day we'll know.

Boot camp training at Parris Island and San Diego is not as heavily involved in combat techniques as is officer training at Quantico. Enlisted Marines will get their combat training

A Few Good Memories

(currently called Infantry Combat Training or ICT) after boot camp at Camp Pendleton and Camp Lejeune. However, officer or enlisted, everyone learns to perform with the same intensity.

Quantico concentrates heavily upon combat training, because when an officer completes the seven months, he or she must be qualified to go directly into a field unit and take command of a platoon. If we're involved in a wartime situation, this officer is expected to be ready immediately. In peacetime, the officer will work with his troops, day after day after day, practicing, training, and getting the platoon ready for the day they'll be called upon.

New officers spend seven or more months at Quantico, at least half of which is fieldwork. They stay in the field—day and night. They endure long (20-mile) marches. They brave the cold of winter and the heat of summer on short marches. In every case, these marches are not simply starting at point A and stopping at point B. These marches have purpose and in most cases are tactical marches, simulating battlefield conditions. Sometimes they will engage in administrative marches, simply a point-to-point non-tactical movement having the purpose of getting troops from Point A to Point B.

As exhausted and tired as these young, soon-to-be leaders become on these tactical movements, some degree of levity exists.

The following story comes from Patrick W. Pat was a former Marine Corps officer and platoon leader. As is the case with many of the stories in this book, Patrick uses a fictitious name for the officer candidate in his story:

> *Wild animals sense weakness in other creatures. Similar behavior in seen in humans also, particularly when the pack is undergoing physical and mental stress, such as in the weight of Marine Corps boot camp.*
>
> *Adams was a fellow officer candidate in my OCS platoon at Quantico in 1958. Every day a newly assigned set of "candidate" leaders took charge. This, of course, was to provide leadership practice for the candidates and insight for the staff to grade our leadership qualities.*

Adams had none of the qualities that we felt were necessary for him to become a Marine officer. We didn't discuss it much; it was just evident.

We were about three-quarters through the course when our syllabus called for an overnight tactical field problem. Our entire training company of three platoons were to force-march about ten miles to a training area and set up a night defense around the crest of a hill. Adams was our candidate platoon leader for the operation.

We arrived at the training area early in the afternoon. Our DI took us to "our hill" and ordered Adams to design and organize our platoon's perimeter defense. Adams was to supervise our defensive setup. Then all of the staff officers and DIs of the company would inspect each candidate's position in the morning. A grade would be assigned. The staff officers and NCO's always seem to end any instructional session with, "A grade will be assigned."

The staff obviously knew about this location and selected it just for us, because it was almost solid rock. All through the night the sounds of entrenching tools, trying to grind their way into the solid rock, pierced the silence of the night.

At 0500, our platoon miserably failed the staff inspection of our positions. Few holes were more than ankle deep. I tried to scrunch and rivet myself down into a four-inch deep hole. I was royally reprimanded, using the DI's reasoning that I would take the first enemy round once the battle started.

Then each member of our platoon evaluated each other's foxhole, specifically estimating the occupant's likely survival in case of an enemy attack. Denunciations from the staff soon died down and we marched to the chow area.

At 0645, the candidate platoon leaders were alerted with a signal from a police whistle from the staff tent area. This meant they were to double-time to the staff HQ for a briefing on the ten-mile return march. Our candidate platoon leader, Adams, double-timed to the HQ area.

A Few Good Memories

As Adams left our bivouac area, our devious minds went to work. We decorated the poor guy's pack and his helmet with at least a hundred dandelions we found growing in the area. I was acting platoon guide and would help him on with his helmet and pack, as well as try to hide the decorations.

Soon he came rushing back, screaming, "OK, guys. Saddle up! Prepare to move out!" As if we were good boys, we all pitched in and helped Adams on with his pack and helmet. And we did a good job of hiding the flowers.

Adams seemed grateful for our sudden assistance. The platoon formed up in two columns. We followed Adams along the path toward the front of the staff HQ tent. All of the staff officers and NCOs stood in review.

We were about fifteen feet away from the staff tent when every officer and NCO, with knowing glances, began shouting things like, "Adams! Get over here!" and "Third platoon! Hold up!"

Adams, the poor guy, had no idea of his predicament until the NCOs snatched his pack and his helmet off and began to grind the flowers in his face. With a soulful and pitiful expression on his face he looked back at us and helplessly uttered something like, "You guys."

A Footnote on Adams:

Two weeks later, Adams got into a shouting match with a staff corporal living in a section of the same barracks as we. Adams had washed his clothes and put them in one of the big rollout steam dryers. Candidates and staff enlisted personnel shared the few washers and dryers, so even on weekends, access was difficult.

The corporal had finished his wash and needed a dryer. None was available except that Adams' dryer had stopped, but he was nowhere in sight. The corporal removed and folded Adams' clothes, then put his own articles in the dryer. This was not unusual because of the limited time and space.

A Few Good Memories

Adams eventually came in and saw what the corporal had done. He began to severely reprimand him. The corporal did not take kindly to this harassment from this officer candidate, and stood his ground. In utter frustration, Adams issued the ultimate threat, "Just wait until I get to be an officer. I'll get you."

On Monday morning, during bayonet-training exercise, Adams was called out of class and sent to the company office. That was the last we saw of him. Soon, we all realized that his rage had dealt the death knell for him, even though, kindly, his name was never mentioned.

A Few Good Memories

18: Gung-Ho Events

The phrase, "Gung Ho," has been applied to Marines for many years. To Marines, this phrase conjures up eagerness, enthusiasm, and zealousness; and must not indicate over-eagerness, over-enthusiasm, or over-zealousness. Well-trained Marines understand that the "over" prefix is a danger to any mission.

A movie produced during World War II touted the Marine Corps in a film, *Gung Ho*. Seeing the film gave me my first inclination that someday I wanted be one of them. Marines in that movie fought the Japanese with all the eagerness, enthusiasm, and zealousness the producers could demonstrate.

The word actually came from the Chinese many years ago. They used the term "kung ho" to indicate togetherness, especially as related to battle. Again, togetherness is a Marine characteristic. Marines are not a "Corps of One," but more like the slogan of the "Three Musketeers," *One for all, and All for One*.

This chapter lumps four training events into one, entitled, "Gung-Ho Events." Each event requires toughness, strength, ability, and just plain guts. Here, Marines learn the basics of what might be experienced later, on the battlefield.

A Few Good Memories

Pugil Sticks

A pugil stick is an innocent-looking article. At first glance, seeing all the padding, one might think fighting with these weapons is a bit of kid's play. It doesn't appear so terrible until you've gone a round with a worthy opponent.

The pugil stick is actually a four-foot long, 12-pound hickory stick. Each end is padded with protective covers. Hand guards allow the recruit to hold the weapon properly. The uniform for participants includes football helmets, a mask, a crotch cover, and a rubber neck-pad.

The fighting area is a circle of sand surrounded by yellow-painted old automobile tires. The two fighting recruits take their places in center ring and await the DI's whistle to start the match. All the other recruits delight in screaming fight commands as the two combatants slug it out.

The object of the pugil stick event is for two participants to engage in close-in combat against each other. Offensively, a contestant tries to club his opponent. Defensively, a contestant tries to protect from being struck. If a competitor is overly concerned offensively, he or she is laid open to attack from the opponent. Conversely, if a competitor is overly concerned with defense, he or she cannot strike the opponent and win. One contestant wins when he or she strikes a clean hit to the head or the neck. This exercise is designed to develop self-confidence, upper body strength, and an aggressive spirit when involved in a fight. Drill instructors are always present and will not hesitate to stop a match immediately.

As might be expected, recruits sometimes become a bit over-zealous and fail to quit when the DI blows his whistle to stop the battle.

This did happen when Bill Y. was a recruit at San Diego Recruit Depot in 1959:

A Few Good Memories

We'd been in boot camp for about nine weeks when our DI told us we had pugil sticks on the schedule. Everybody had been waiting for this, and I think I was too. This would be a way for us to get rid of some of our frustrations.

They told us how to do pugil sticks. One DI talked while some of the DIs put on the gear and went through some of the moves. It looked like fun and everybody was getting excited.

I was paired with this recruit named Don. He was a good guy and real quiet. I was worried because he was a lot smaller than I was and I didn't want to hurt him. I figured that he'd just try to keep out of my way as much as he could.

The DI called all the teams to the center. Don and I got in position and the DI blew his whistle. I didn't want to whack Don too hard, so I just parried a little bit. All of a sudden here came Don. Before I knew it he was fighting like a fighting cock. I was a pretty good fighter so I started fighting back. This seemed to get up his dander and I saw his eyes narrow down. The DIs told us we weren't supposed to "take it out" on our sparring partners. I think Don did.

Next thing I knew he had put a real hit to my head and I kind of blacked out a little bit. I did hear the DI's whistle, but Don kept coming and hitting. He got another good lick in before the DI's jumped on him.

The DIs pulled him over to the side and calmed him down. After a little while they asked me if I wanted another match with him. They said they had explained how the system works and he said he understands. I said OK.

We fought again. I protected myself well and didn't let Don get to me like he did the first time. Don did get the best of me, but this time he followed the rules and stopped when the whistle blew.

I did figure out one thing: If we ever have the opportunity to go into battle, I want Don by my side!

A Few Good Memories

Confidence Course

They call it the Confidence Course. Sometimes it seems more like the "Impossible Course." Every phase of recruit training teaches something new. Each phase is designed to prove to a recruit that he or she has what it takes to be a Marine, if they can just get through this phase. Recruits know that every phase must be completed or they'll never make it to the eagle, globe, and anchor ceremony; when they become Marines.

The confidence course proves to recruits that they have the capacity to deal with difficult tasks. It's composed of a series of activities including leg-building, upper-body strength, endurance, and working at steep heights. Different obstacles are encountered. Events include climbing high log crossbeams, traveling by the use of ropes, scaling high walls, and jumping water obstacles.

Another event is called the Slide for Life. One hundred or so feet of rope is stretched from the top of a tower down to a creek below. Recruits hold onto the rope and slide, while maintaining control and landing fully ready to fight.

The Hand Walk is another grueling event. At first sight this looks easy. Actually, this double set of steel pipes, with cross pipes making a long ladder-like structure, starts at about six feet up, winds around, down, up, and over for more than 30 feet, sometimes over a grimy, dirty, and mucky pool. The recruit is not allowed to touch the deck with his or her feet, hands, or anything else. What began as a snap, becomes an exhausting journey.

Read this story from Oscar R. about a recruit who wanted to complete the Hand Walk but couldn't do it. They sent him through several times, but he didn't succeed until the DIs convinced him he could:

I went through San Diego Boot Camp in 1986. We had this recruit, Watson, in our platoon. He was a little guy. He was a good guy. Sometimes all the others in our platoon wished we could help him with stuff where more height was needed.

We were at the Confidence Course on our final run for test. Watson was doing OK at first. He was small, so some of the things were a lot harder for him than for some of us tall guys.

He did OK on the Slide for Life and the things before it, but then he got to the Hand Walk. He had just plain given out. Anyway, he jumped up to the first cross pipe and started hand-over-hand. His movement slowed down so that when he got halfway, dead over the water, he was about ready to drop. He just hung there.

The DIs started yelling for him to get out of the way. "If you can't hack it, clear the way!" they'd yell. He tried again and again. Watson knew if he dropped he'd have to start all over, and he was so tired he'd never make it even this far next time.

Finally, one of the DIs yelled at him, "You finish it this time and I'll do the Hand Walk. When I get over the water I'll fall, intentionally."

All us recruits started yelling at Watson to go. We wanted to see the DI mired in the mud. The little guy got some strength from somewhere and slowly made his way—all the way to the end! DIs and recruits alike yelled and clapped. True to his word, like a Marine always is, the DI did his Hand Walk, got over the muck, and dropped. That was when I knew I'd follow that DI to the end of the earth.

Gas Chamber

The name, "Gas Chamber," creates eerie thoughts in the minds of recruits. World War I gave the world its first real encounters with this terrible—and illegal under the terms of the Geneva Convention—weapon. Although the United States loathes the idea of using gas, we must be prepared for the possibility that recruits might one day be confronted with it.

On gas chamber day, recruits gather at the Chamber as the last event of the day. A comprehensive pre-gas session teaches them how to put on a gas mask properly. They learn to fit the mask closely to their skin. A small leakage on the battlefield could be deadly, according to the type of gas used.

With the demonstration over, all the recruits remove their masks and are moved through a small door and into the chamber. A dim light is turned on. The door is closed. Can you imagine a more uncanny feeling?

One of the DIs reaches up and turns a handle. A small jet of gas comes in. This gas is a simple gas—tear gas, which is used for riot control. It's called CS. The gas is non-lethal, except that it'll burn a bit and tear your eyes.

"Gas!" yells the DI. That's the battlefield alert that says, "Masks on!" Some recruits calmly slip the mask over their faces. Others panic, causing them to fumble. The longer they wait, the more CS burns. Most recruits succeed. Those that didn't, go back for a second try. This time most of the recruits succeed.

The walk back to the barracks clears the nostrils and the throats of these recruits, but they have learned the importance of a gas mask.

Rifle Range

Recruits, male and female, are required to qualify with the basic infantry rifle used by the Marine Corps at that time. In my day it was the M-1. We have progressed to the M16A2, a super weapon capable of delivering at least ten times the firepower as the M-1 of my day.

Whatever the weapon, recruits are anxious. They look forward to qualifying and wearing their badge, the rifle qualification badge. They want the world to learn of their accomplishments. It's often the first subject out of the new Marine's mouth back home.

Every recruit must qualify; no question about it. Whether he or she will be in an infantry rifle platoon or working on the flight line, qualification is a requirement.

Retired MSGT Peter W. sent in this story about the rifle range. The master sergeant spent 28 years in the Corps. Most of that time he had been an armorer or a rifle range NCO. Here is his story about an incident on the range at Parris Island:

The rifle range was always pretty good duty, because afternoons were usually pretty quiet. This story is about a Thursday morning on the rifle range down at Parris Island in the spring during the seventies. We had been firing for a little over an hour that morning. The recruits on the line were doing pretty well and were on the 300-yard line preparing for 300-yard-line rapid fire, from the prone position.

Down on the right end, I kept seeing maggie's drawers; lots of them. Every "maggie's drawer" flag meant a miss. That recruit on the end was having a real problem. They were supposed to shoot for record the next day. This would be a catastrophe. I always prided myself on "my" recruits shooting good scores. I thought maybe the recruit's DI would be working with him but he wasn't. I told one of my range NCOs to go over and check it out.

My NCO came back and showed me the recruit's score. Every shot was a miss. Never in the history of the rifle range, especially my rifle range, had anybody ever shot zero. But that seemed to be where we were headed. I'd be the laughing stock.

We finished the 300-yard line and moved back to the 500 for slow fire. The same thing happened there: maggie's drawers on every shot. I was a nervous wreck.

Finally, the last shot went off on the 500-yard line. I yelled "Cease fire," and climbed down from the tower. I stormed over to the recruit. Then I heard, "April Fool," in a loud chorus. Then I realized it. It was April 1. The "recruit" on the end was actually one of the DIs from the recruit's platoon. Everybody, including the range officer, had set me up. And I was never able to live it down. Damn guys.

Rappelling Tower

The shortest distance between two points is a straight line, according to engineers and mathematicians. No person or group that I know of has ever proposed to contradict that theorem. Maybe this is the theory that formed the basis for the Marine Corps' use of rappelling to rapidly descend from a high point to a low point.

Rappelling is a "required course" in Marine Corps boot camp. Not only will many of these recruits use this maneuver in the future as ground troops, but it also is an effective confidence builder. The first time most recruits climb to the top of the 40-foot rappelling tower at Parris Island and look over the side, they are virtually frightened to death. Forty feet, looking down, is a much greater distance than forty feet looking up!

Before recruits even touch the rappelling tower, they practice all of the basic rappelling moves on the ground. Drill instructors work for hours teaching them how to hold the ropes, how to control descent, and how to maintain stability, and what to do in case of trouble.

After groundwork, recruits move to a low tower where they practice short-distance ascents and descents. They gain confidence as they progress to higher and more difficult events. Then before they realize it, they are on the high tower, ready to rappel. As recruits descend the tower, drill instructors are always at their sides, encouraging each to finish. Every recruit *must* satisfactorily complete the rappelling event before the day is over.

A Few Good Memories

Michael M. was a recruit in 1977. Here is his story about the day his platoon conquered the rappelling tower:

It was a pretty cold day in February 1977, when we marched to the rappelling tower. Two other male platoons and a female platoon joined us. Everything seemed to go fine, except for one female recruit who appeared to be the only failure for the day. She was so frightened that she froze about midway down the tower. Two drill instructors stayed beside her, shouting helpful and encouraging comments. We all thought she was going to fall. We wondered why the DIs didn't help her down. But they couldn't actually help her or it wouldn't count. Suddenly, all of the 240 recruits on the ground started yelling for her and shouted for her to go, go, go.

It must have worked. She seemed to gain her confidence and started a slow and deliberate descent. Shouts and applause from the other recruits grew louder. She kept coming down. As she reached the ground, drill instructors and recruits alike showered her with an ovation hard to believe—a showering display of camaraderie.

The recruit was so overwhelmed that she asked to go up and come down again. Her request was approved and she ran every step up to the top of the tower. Two drill instructors accompanied her. This time her descent was almost a picture book effort.

Talk about a confidence builder! No doubt that the Corps understands what they are doing as they design events that build each individual's self-confidence. This story also represents the spirit of teamwork that is embedded deeply inside every recruit who leaves boot camp.

A Few Good Memories

19: The Crucible

Arthur Miller's 1953 book, *The Crucible*, was supposedly inspired by the so-called reign of terror caused by the anti-Communist hearings held by Senator Joseph McCarthy. Without stirring up a political whirlwind, I will only suggest that the name for the last phase of boot camp probably came from Miller's book.

Every new Marine since 1997 has endured this final test. Soon-to-be-Marines are spared no hardship during this 54-hour ordeal that evaluates every recruit physically, mentally, and morally. Up until now, recruits have fended for themselves, succeeding or failing on their own merits and abilities or lack thereof.

The Crucible takes the already-tough boot camp regimen to a new level. Recruits must help each other, advise one another, and think as a team to pass this final exam. No one member can succeed for the team. A group effort is essential.

The final exam has no answer sheet. In every event assigned to the recruits, the result is either pass or fail. Reaching the goal means the whole team succeeds. Failure to accomplish the mission means the entire team fails.

General Charles C. Krulak, Commandant of the Marine Corps, conceived of the idea to add the Crucible to an already-tough training regimen in order to prepare the Corps for its role in

A Few Good Memories

the 21st century. He felt that a heightened sense of Core Values (honor, courage, and commitment) within each new Marine would be reached by adding this extraordinary last phase of training.

The heart of the Crucible is teamwork. The Marine Corps is unique in the efficiency of its chain of command. Many years ago, the Corps found that in the throes of battle it is very difficult for a single leader to control more than three subordinates. Thus the *fire team* originated. Typically, a Marine Corps fire team is composed of a fire team leader (corporal) and three subordinates. A squad is composed of a squad leader and three fire teams. Three squads and a platoon commander make up a platoon. A company contains three platoons and is commanded by the company commander. A battalion is composed of three companies and a battalion commander. Three battalions make up a regiment. A division contains three regiments.

This schematic is much different from the fighting commands of the early days of this country. In Colonial days, hundreds of men lined up shoulder to shoulder with raised muskets. They loaded and delivered fusillades of fire upon the commands of their few officers on horseback. As men on the front rank fell, the second rank took their places. The side that had men remaining on the field won these human slaughters. Strangely enough, one significant rule of ethics existed. Soldiers were expected not to fire at the opposing officers.

I met in the Thomasville, Georgia, Marine Corps recruiting office to get a first-hand account of the Crucible. Pvt. Billy Grant was temporarily assigned there to help with recruiting of new candidates. With Billy being fresh out of boot camp, I looked to him for an up-to-the-minute update. He did a good job.

Reveille goes at 0230. For non-military types, this is 2:30 in the morning. Field packs are donned for the forced march to the training area. Upon arrival, the DIs get in a few minutes of administrative time to let recruits know what is to occur.

The Crucible is conducted with recruits broken into fire teams. Each fire team must complete eight problem events. Each event has a starting point and a goal, but no "school solution." The fire team decides how to accomplish the goal. The plan must be made quickly. These are timed events.

A Few Good Memories

The fire team passes an event if and only if it accomplishes its goal within the time allotted. Each member of the fire team is assigned as leader for two events. All events are simulated. Rifles are loaded with blank ammunition. Explosive charges detonate continuously throughout the conduct of the Crucible. DIs are present at all times to ensure safety.

Event 1 is a rescue from a crashed helicopter. An injured man is trapped inside. The enemy is firing on the fire team and is expected to attack quickly. The goal is to extricate the injured man and carry him to safety without losing either him or the fire team.

Event 2 is a movement through a simulated jungle. Periodically the fire team will run into a blocked passage and will have to turn back. The object is to make it through the maze. The tough part is that once the team backs out of a passage, it must try to remember which passages are blocked.

Event 3 is an attempt to get a vehicle tire over a 12-feet high obstacle. No ladders, ropes, poles, or other forms of leverage are available. The tire must be raised and lowered without tossing or dropping. Most teams end up with two members standing on the shoulders of the other two members.

In **Event 4**, recruits cross a chasm by using a series of ropes. This requires a highly organized team effort. Four ropes hang from a beam above and are spaced about 12 feet apart. The fire team begins by swinging on Rope One from Landing One to the second landing, 12 feet away. The rope is tossed back to the starting point where the next member grabs it and commences swinging to follow the leader. By this time the leader is swinging to the third landing. Now three recruits are aboard the ropes and the fourth member is preparing to swing. Every member must pass each rope accurately and grab each rope for the event to work.

Event 5 is called the spider web with bells. The goal is to pass a buddy through a six-feet-high hole in the web-like series of ropes to the other side ... without ringing the bells. Ringing the bells will alert the "enemy."

Event 6, the tank walk, requires on a great deal of teamwork. The fire team lines up in column formation with about a one-foot separation between recruits. Two ropes, one on each side, are tied so that the recruits' toes are fastened to the ropes. The fire team proceeds, creeping down a track of about 20 feet—all lefts, then all rights—in unison, lest the entire team tumbles.

Event 7 is a difficult obstacle course. Included are the rope climb and the "stairway to heaven," a 50-feet high ladder. To negotiate this stairway requires that recruits assist one another at the highest level.

Event 8 is called ditch movement. Blanks are loaded in the M-16 rifles. Recruits move up, one at a time, firing at pre-positioned targets. When a target is 'hit,' the concussion from the fired blank knocks it out of commission. That recruit then drops to the deck, covering while the next recruit moves up into the next firing position. Missing a target is a failed event. The team must restart.

These events would be difficult enough in broad daylight, but most of them occur during the dark of the night. Inclement weather does not cancel the Crucible. It's the luck of the draw if it rains.

Now the good part begins. The "hump," as it is called, is the long march back after so many hours of sleep and food deprivation. When the forced march begins, invariably a recruit begins singing The Marine Corps Hymn. It's like a cue for the rest. All the way home, verse after verse of the Hymn, yelling, screaming, proud.

The class gathers in formation on the parade ground for the moment they've all waited for; the *EGA ceremony*. Each recruit is awarded the Eagle, Globe, and Anchor pin from his or her drill instructor. The sounds of "Congratulations, Marine," echo loudly across the parade ground as the DIs shake the hand of each new Marine. Prior to this moment, they were recruits, ineligible to be called Marines, ineligible to shake the hand of the DI. This is the moment that each recruit realizes that he or she would follow the DI into the depths of Hell itself.

With their new pins in hand, the recruits file into the mess hall. No longer must they remain silent during the meal. They are Marines. They eat the *Warriors Breakfast*, all they want this time—eggs, bacon, sausage, potatoes, pancakes, bear claws, milk, juice, toast, name it. In some cases, it's served by their DIs.

The new Marines have passed the final test, the defining moment. The Corps remains alive and well. And a new class starts next week.

20: Graduation

Graduation week is a most welcomed time. If a recruit is still with it until that last week or so, he or she can be fairly certain that success is just over the ridge. But still, plenty of work remains. The parade must go according to plan. Why? The general will probably be there. And all those parents! The graduation ceremony is not something to mess up. Plenty of practice is necessary to be sure that everyone knows exactly where to go, what to do, and when to do it.

The parade is not the only item on the agenda that should be perfect. The recruits themselves must show perfection. Every day (sometimes twice a day) the DIs inspect, inspect, inspect. They'll stand on the quarterdeck with all recruits at attention and call out a uniform type. The next command will give the time that the recruits are allowed to change and be in formation.

This graduation drill is not only practiced at Parris Island and San Diego. Quantico does it too. Just ask Leo Switzer. He was an officer candidate in June 1955 at Quantico. Leo's platoon was involved in this quick-change exercise. Read his story:

A Few Good Memories

It was the middle of June, two weeks before my graduation from Quantico as a Marine officer—a brand new second lieutenant. Thirty-four candidates had started this twelve-week plague. Now, twenty of us remained. Periodically, during the past few weeks, a candidate would quietly disappear. No goodbyes. No beer party. We knew the staff officers were weeding us out; it was nerve-wracking. Who'd be next?

On this Saturday morning our schedule provided two hours of early-morning graduation practice drill, then two hours of inside classes. After noon chow, about 1330 hours, our drill instructor, SSgt Weinach, marched us onto the grinder. He said that his platoon was going to win the company drill competition and be the sharpest looking platoon on the field, if we had to practice twenty-four hours a day. And he meant it.

First he would carry out one of his meticulous inspections. A speck of dust on a rifle was a cardinal sin. Every shoe must shine so perfectly that he could see his face. I thought I was ready.

I wasn't. Just before we fell into formation, the uniform for drill practice changed at least three times. First, it was khaki with no ribbons. Then it was dungarees. The last change was khaki, and whether or not to wear the National Defense Service Ribbon affixed over our left pockets. Most of the time, every man seemed to end up in the proper uniform for drill practice.

Slowly SSgt Weinach made his way down the front rank. His piercing eagle eyes looked me over. He slowly drew his k-bar, or longknife as he called it, from its scabbard, and raised it toward my throat. I thought I was a goner. He stuck the k-bar under my field scarf (tie) and flipped it up, revealing that in the haste of pinning on the ribbon, I had failed to re-button one of my shirt buttons.

Weinach made a production out of my blunder. He called the candidate platoon leader and my candidate squad leader over and chewed them out because of my appearance. Then he grabbed my button in one hand and sawed it off my shirt with his k-bar. He formed the entire platoon into a circle and dropped the button onto the concrete deck. Slowly, with powerful strokes, he pounded it into a fine white powder with the butt-end of his k-bar.

The angry DI then ordered the platoon back into formation, and with a great amount of formality, ordered me to restore the button to its original state. He reminded me that if I wanted to be a Marine I would find a way to follow every order. I had five minutes to put that button back together.

It wasn't funny to me, but Skip, my good friend and the candidate standing next to me, snickered aloud. Suddenly the DI's emphasis moved from me to Skip for a moment. Weinach chewed on Skip for a while. As if a chewing out wasn't enough, Skip was ordered to assist me in the resurrection of the button. The rest of the platoon was marched back onto the grinder to practice close-order drill.

In spite of our diligent efforts, Skip and I did not succeed. For some strange reason we could not resurrect that button. I was sure I would suffer the ultimate penalty for my failure and "just disappear" from the scene like so many others had. Skip and I did survive, however, and we earned our second lieutenant gold bars. But even today, over forty years later, I still double-check my shirt buttons.

A Few Good Memories

21: Home

Harry D. was proud to be a new Marine and to talk of his rifle range exploits. But the following story shows that it doesn't always turn out exactly as intended:

I was proud of myself. I had finished boot camp and was home to see the family. Uncles, a brother, aunts, sisters, and even my girl friend, were at the supper. They asked a million questions a minute, and I tried to answer them. My mama was hanging on every word. "Your daddy would have been so proud of you," she said a hundred times.

Edward, my youngest uncle, was a gun nut and he wanted to know how I did at the rifle range. I told him I did OK and I showed him my sharpshooter badge. Everybody turned to listen about how we would shoot and pull butts and shoot some more, and how the range personnel jumped on anyone who didn't follow the rules. I told them that I might have shot "expert" except that I had this accidental discharge on the firing line one day and the range people stayed on my case the rest of the week.

A Few Good Memories

Mama piped up. In trying to make me feel better she said, "Harry, you got to remember that that can happen to any young man, especially when he's not married yet. Don't worry yourself about it."

That broke up the party and they're all still laughing about it after twelve years!

A Few Good Memories

Appendix 1

The Drill Instructor

Once the preliminaries are over, the recruit platoon is up to strength. They have received their gear and are raring to get started. Some have dropped out for various reasons—medical, psychological, or personal. It's time for the remaining 60 or so recruits to meet their drill instructors. Their DIs will be with them every minute for the next 12 weeks. They will be their fathers, their mothers, their nemeses; and at the end of the 12 weeks, their heroes.

To be a DI, a Marine must graduate from Drill Instructor School, an intense 12-week course that teaches the theory of education as it applies to the boot camp. It fills in the gaps left by poorly prepared parents and ineffective schoolteachers.

Drill Instructor candidates are selected from the best Marines in the field. Currently, to be selected, a candidate must be at the rank of sergeant or above, have an exemplary record, and be recommended by his or her commanding officer.

DI School is tough. Not every Marine can be a drill instructor. Not every DI candidate will graduate from Drill Instructor School. In fact, usually only seven of 10 candidates have what it takes to be a DI and earn that coveted DI cover (hat). It is a tough course. Not only must the Marine be physically capable of doing the job—most are—but the candidate must also show an ability to motivate recruits and to instill core values that all Marines must possess.

The making of a Marine in today's Corps is a lot different from the Corps of 50 years ago. Today, politicians, mothers, congressmen, and all sorts of barriers blunt the Corps' ability to concentrate on making Marines the way they once did. But given these limitations, external qualifying factors and conditions, these outstanding drill instructors still get the job done. It's a lot tougher, a lot more demanding; and it's a lot riskier to the DI's career. But they are Marines, so they get it done. And that is the foundational reason that the United States Marine Corps is without equal.

Read this story from MSgt. Mark Watkins, USMC (Ret):

I remember DI School well. It was 1984. They sent me to Parris Island to be a DI. I had mixed emotions. I'd heard how tough DI School is. I'd heard that the slightest error might ruin your career. Oh, what the hell, I thought. I can use the extra few bucks each payday.

I got the education of my life. We studied first aid, military history, Marine Corps history, the Marine Corps Guidebook, and psychology (a lot of psychology). We worked night and day. We ran the obstacle course till we knew it by heart. We did sit-ups, push-ups, twists, leg lifts, mountain climbers, and side-straddle hops. We did stuff that have no names. We worked in the combat pool. I ended up in the best shape of my life.

We learned how to handle touchy recruit situations. We learned how to handle them so it would help both the recruit and us. We all agreed that a DI should get a psychology degree when he finished. I think we got that right.

We took turns drilling our platoon till we were blue in the face. We stood inspections. We learned the real way to handle a rifle when we inspected. We learned how to handle panic attacks on the rifle range. We had junk-on-the-bunk inspections. We conducted junk-on-the-bunk inspections.

Our DI School instructors treated us like recruits, the worst of recruits. They tried to break us. And some did break. When they did, they were gone by sundown.

A Few Good Memories

I had always said that Marine Corps boot camp was the hardest thing I'd ever done in my life. Forget that. Drill Instructor School was by far the hardest thing I've ever done in my life.

I graduated and spent the remainder of my three-year tour at Parris Island as a DI. It showed new light on the Corps. I went through 11 cycles. I was Third Hat for two cycles, Second Hat for five, then Senior Drill Instructor for four cycles.

I was promoted to gunnery sergeant a few months before my DI tour was up. I was glad to get back to Camp Pendleton. My wife was glad to get back to Pendleton. She said now I could get to know my young son.

I joined the 7th Marines as a company gunnery sergeant. I had former recruits coming to me with "Hey, Gunny. Remember me?" It made me feel good to see those wide grins and their full respect. It also made me feel good to know I was hard on these kids. If I have to go into battle with them, I want them trained right.

Jim D. is one of those "Types A's" to whom we owe a tremendous amount of thanks and gratitude. He entered boot camp during a critical period in the history of this country. We were in the beginning of World War II and whether the Axis powers of Germany and Japan would conquer the United States was very much in doubt. America's young people flocked to the recruiting stations. And thank God they did. This is Jim's story about his memory of his DI:

On August 12, 1943, my platoon graduated from Parris Island. Boot camp had been shortened to only eight weeks. The drill instructors reminded us again and again that the Marine Corps needed "bullet sponges" on the beaches of the South Pacific. These words were not very comforting to green, untrained boots, but we were kept too busy to let it sink in.

A Few Good Memories

Boot camp drill instructors were hated, adored, and envied. It all depended on the stage of training. For the first third of training, a boot promises himself that one day he will kill his DI. At the mid-point of training, the recruit begins building a resistance to the constant terror and frustration. He makes up his mind that he can take anything those SOB drill instructors can dish out. Finally, on graduation day, the DI is the hero of every Marine in the platoon. These new Marines would follow this leader to the ends of the earth, obeying every command with dedication.

We were not allowed to eat pogey bait (candy, soft drinks, snacks,etc). Often when our platoon marched past the PX, the drill instructor would taunt us with, "Hey, Ladies. You want some pogey bait?" Naturally, we would yell in the affirmative, even though we knew we'd never see any of those sweet and desirable chocolate bars.

One hot day in August, as our platoon passed the PX, the DI bellowed his, "You want pogey bait?" Everyone responded with, "YES SIR!" We couldn't believe it when he halted the platoon.

"OK, you clowns. Have at it. Two minutes. Eat all you damn well please."

We wolfed down candy bars and sodas. Two minutes later, the DI reformed the platoon and we continued our run. In no time, we were heaving and throwing up. Some fell to the ground. The stomach pain was unbearable. The DI did not let up. He'd say, "Come on ladies, you wanted the stuff. Now move!"

The next stop was sick bay, not because we were pogey-bait-sick, but because this was the day our platoon had been scheduled to receive tetanus shots; and a little thing like heaving and throwing up was not going to stop that.

Afterwards, we double-timed to a sandy training area, where we engaged in two hours of rigorous bayonet drill. The final scheduled activity for the day was the obstacle course. This time, instead of the usual two to three times through the course, the drill instructor sent us through five times.

I still remember that day every time I pass the candy section at the grocery store and inhale the sweet aroma of caramel, chocolate, and jelly beans. But I especially remember Snicker bars. I dug in my pocket that day, pulled out my last forty-five cents, bought, and ate nine *cherished Snickers.*

The S*enior Drill Instructor* (SDI) is usually a gunnery sergeant or sometimes a senior staff sergeant. He or she has had the experience of several cycles of boots and has the overall responsibility for the training of the platoon. The SDI will dish out discipline when needed, help with training, or, in rare cases, will extend a shoulder to a recruit. The SDI's job is to graduate as many *qualified* recruits as possible.

Second in command is usually another staff sergeant called the S*econd Hat.* The Second Hat, sometimes called the Heavy A, handles special training situations. Often a recruit cannot develop the correct rhythm for drill movements. The Heavy A will take the recruit aside for individual training.

Third in the chain of command is the *Third Hat*. The Third Hat is usually a junior staff sergeant or a sergeant. This will be his or her first or second cycle. In cases where strong discipline is required the Third Hat takes over.

The rules governing the duties for each DI are not hard and fast. Each DI will do whatever is necessary to help turn those inept recruits into Marines. Their actual duties may overlap as directed by the SDI.

One other Marine is included in the immediate chain of command for recruits. This person is a commissioned officer, usually a first lieutenant with the title of S*eries Officer.* He or she is responsible for one or more recruit platoons. The first time that the recruits see the SO is when he or she administers the Drill Instructor Oath to the DIs, loudly, so all may hear:

A Few Good Memories

Drill Instructor's Pledge

These recruits are entrusted to my care. I will train them to the best of my ability. I will develop them into smartly disciplined, physically fit, basically trained Marines, thoroughly indoctrinated in love of Corps and country. I will demand of them, and demonstrate by my own example, the highest standards of personal conduct, morality and professional skill.

The SDI works under the eye of, and reports to, the SO. After that first meeting, recruits have little close contact with the officer, except in special or serious cases. This is structured so that when contact is necessary, it can be more meaningful.

On the afternoon of December 6, 1999, I visited Major B. R. Gerstbrein, officer in charge of the Parris Island Drill Instructor School. This stop was not originally on my itinerary, but a few days before going to Parris Island, I read his letter, which is posted on the PI web site, **www.parrisisland.com**, to Marines reporting in for DI School. His letter impressed me. I made a request and was granted an interview with the major.

During our interview, Major Gerstbrein eloquently stated his philosophy of the training of the trainers, of how to motivate the motivators. In that few hours, in the company of the major, I understood why all is well in the Corps. I understood why fathers of all recruits should be pleased. I understood why all mothers should be overjoyed for the transformation that is taking place at this very moment of their sons and daughters.

Below are excerpts from the Major's open letter to Marines attending DI School:

Congratulations on your selection to attend Drill Instructor School. You are about to embark upon one of the most rewarding experiences of your entire Marine Corps career. Most students find this course physically and professionally challenging and fulfilling. It will greatly expand your horizons as a professional Non-commissioned Officer and Staff Non-commissioned Officer, as well as prepare you for your tour as a Drill Instructor.

Upon completion of your tour as a Drill Instructor, you will return to the Fleet Marine Force a more knowledgeable and self-confident Marine leader, fully capable of assuming any billet or completing any mission assigned.

The one thing that distinguishes the Marine Corps from any other armed force in the world is our recruit training. The individual most responsible for conducting that training and providing that inspiring leadership is the Drill Instructor. The staff and I firmly believe that the future of our Corps rests on the shoulders of our graduates.

Do not take the rigors of Drill Instructor School lightly. Substantial demands will be made of you. Physical and mental preparation is the key to success!

Semper Fi,
Major B. R. Gerstbrein
Director, Drill Instructor School

Major Gerstbrein's top assistant was First Sergeant E. M. Brisbin, the Chief Instructor at Drill Instructor School. First Sgt Brisbin's message to DI School students is demanding in philosophy. The following are excerpts from his message:

The Drill Instructor is the first Marine a recruit meets when reporting for active duty. He is the last Marine the recruit should ever forget. The drill instructor is the role model that will be forever emulated by the recruits. Drill Instructor School graduates must understand that they will have a critical impact on the future of the Marine Corps.

A Few Good Memories

You must be able to assimilate instruction, prioritize tasks, and simultaneously manage many responsibilities.

Accordingly, your time management skills will dictate your ability to handle the curriculum. You must be determined and have a positive attitude at all times.

A good Marine can be a good drill instructor. If you have the desire to teach, instruct, develop and evaluate personnel, you have indeed chosen the right career path. Bear in mind the magnitude of the responsibilities that you are about to undertake. As a potential drill instructor, you will have the opportunity to join the elite men and women who instill the pride, discipline, and spirit into young recruits, developing them into members of the finest fighting force in the world. Welcome aboard."

First Sergeant E. M. Brisbin
Chief Instructor, Drill Instructor School

Sometimes recruits come to boot camp never having before taken "community showers." At boot camp, it's a new game. Most recruits will plunge right in and forget his or her modesty. George M. was a Senior Drill Instructor at boot camp in 1956. In his platoon he had a very modest recruit:

In 1956, I was a senior DI at MCRD, San Diego. Private showers did not exist.

Dippy, as my fellow DIs and I called this recruit, was one of those modest men in my platoon. Dippy would wait until the very last moment, until he thought most everyone was out of the showers, before he went in. If he found someone there, he would back out and sit on a commode until the coast was clear.

The word soon got around to me. I called Dippy in and asked him about it. Dippy told me that he never had taken a shower with other people before and if he didn't have to, could he get special permission. He even went so far as to offer to do extra cleaning duty at night.

Like all good drill instructors, I felt great compassion for this lowly recruit. First, I threatened to beat him to a pulp. Then I promised to turn him over to one of the South San Diego street gangs. Neither of these threats seemed to be in line with what he thought was best.

Finally, I took it upon myself to solve his problem. The next day at noon chow time, I tramped Dippy into his squad bay and made him take off every stitch of his clothes. I marched him out to the front of the chow hall. I gave him five tickets. Actually they were only small, torn pieces of paper, but what does a maggot know?

I instructed Dippy to run around the parade ground and return to me. Each time he returned I took one of the tickets. When he was out of tickets he could put his clothes on and eat chow. I told Dippy that we would repeat this procedure each noon until he felt inclined to join his platoon at shower time.

The next morning, the entire platoon, including Dippy, had the pleasure to shower together.

Skip H. was a career Marine. He went through Parris Island and learned all the things that recruits should learn to be good Marines. Read his story about shoe dye:

As new recruits at boot camp, we had just been issued our uniforms. For the first few days we wore nothing but our dungarees, also known as utilities, those drab green uniforms in which Marines work out of doors and fight. Other branches of the service call them fatigues, but our drill instructors would not allow us to even think the word.

On Thursday evening the DI came in and ordered us to get ready for inspection the next morning. Uniform would be tropical worsted. We were also to dye our dress shoes from brown to black. We were ordered not to spill a drop of black dye. The DI would monitor us as we worked.

A Few Good Memories

(I always wondered why the Corps had bought brown shoes if they wanted them black.)

One recruit came up with an excellent idea. We should put a swab bucket on the deck, place the bottle of dye inside the bucket, and hold the shoes over the bucket so as not to drop dye on the clean deck.

It worked fine. I was the last recruit to dye shoes. When I finished and started to get up from my campstool, my foot banged the bucket. Thankfully, it had only knocked over the dye bottle. The bucket was still upright.

The DI spotted it—unfortunately, the bucket had a hole in the bottom. Dye ran out through the hole, onto the deck, formed a puddle about two fingers wide, and inched along in a straight line. The DI launched into an everlasting outburst that made me wonder again why I was so ever so stupid to think I was good enough to be a Marine.

For four days, instead of taking advantage of my precious little free time, I had to spend my hours with bleach, soap, and a wire brush, trying to remove the foot-long stain. All I succeeded in doing was to cut a channel into the deck by scrubbing with the brush so hard. The stain would not come out.

A few years later I returned to Parris Island as a drill instructor. I had forgotten the shoe dye incident until one evening it flashed through my mind. I had to look. I went over to my old barracks and checked in with the duty drill instructor to tell him that I wanted to see the deck I had ruined. He grinned and led me into the squad bay. It was still there; not as dark, but the stain was still evident. Nostalgia overtook me as I recalled my battle with the shoe dye.

Drill instructors resist any form of familiarization with recruits. That's the way it must be. In the field of combat, a Marine must follow orders immediately and without question or hesitation. Sometimes the senior drill instructor will become a father, a mother, or a bit of a friend to a recruit, if he or she really needs it. They know when and how to do this. Drill instructors, by reputation, are mean, cranky, cantankerous, uncaring, and all those other words that Marines sometimes use. In reality, the DI wants to make a recruit into the best Marine possible. Once in a blue moon a different story, a compassionate one, surfaces from this "land of terror."

B. Jackson shares this emotional story of his senior drill instructor, a *compassionate* DI:

Most of the recruits in our platoon at San Diego thought our senior drill instructor acted a little strangely. He was a terror in the field, but sometimes he would fall into a protective demeanor during non-training hours. Without warning, he would send for one of us boots to come into his quarters for what he called his support sessions. He never summoned more than one boot at a time. It was usually on Sunday afternoons.

I remember that Sunday afternoon in 1957, when my turn came. Frightened, I rapped on his hatch. He responded with, "Get in here!" I did. There he was. Laid back on a lounge, wearing Marine-green skivvies, the kind that the Corps issued during World War II and Korea. He wore Marine-issue combat boots, every eye-hook laced fully to the top and tied neatly.

"Recruit Jackson reporting as ordered, Sir."

Then I noticed that he was drinking a can of Seven Up soda and eating purple grapes. It almost made me want to throw up, except that I'd have liked to have the soda, but not at the same time as the grapes. I thought the others who'd been there before had been kidding. Seven Up and grapes?

I stood rigidly at attention. Recruits learn that the only legitimate posture is attention unless otherwise instructed. My eyes riveted on a discoloration on the bulkhead straight ahead and at eye level.

"You from Vegas?" He knew I was from Las

Vegas. He always chided me about being from tinsel town.

"Yes, sir!"

"Miss it?"

"No, sir." No way was I going to slightly hint that I'd rather be someplace other than the Marine Corps Recruit Depot in San Diego.

"You don't miss home?"

"No, sir. The Corps is my home now." I figured he'd soak that up and maybe not be so tough next week when we were scheduled for our first week on the rifle range.

"Whatdaya want to do in the Corps, Maggot?"

"I want to be a gravel cruncher, sir. **Oh three**, through and through." I was looking for a brownie point or so by letting him know that I understood that "oh three" meant infantry and I wanted to get my 0311 MOS when I finished Basic Infantry Training up at Camp Pendleton.

"You mean you don't want motor pool?"

"No, sir. I want to fight, not fix. And I'd rather have my hands dirty with mud, not grease."

The sergeant just sat and looked at me, for a good two or three minutes. I remained silent. A boot never speaks until he is given permission.

"Lemme show you something, Jackson. Stand at ease." I couldn't remember when any DI had ever offered me the chance to stand at ease. He unlaced his boots all the way down to the eyelets. "See these boots?"

"Yes, sir, Sergeant."

"Here's the way a real Marine laces his boots." With one hand he grabbed the two lace ends of his left boot, and stretched them outward, parallel to each other about an inch apart. He began to swing his hand to the left, then the right, and back again, so fast I could hardly see what was happening, except that the laces were catching the eye-hooks with each movement of his hand. In seconds the boot was laced and tied.

I was definitely impressed. He must have realized it. Then in a further display of his coordination and hand-deftness, with both hands he laced both boots at the same time. He smiled and asked, "You think you'll ever be able to do that?"

"I'm not sure, sir."

Years later, I was a sergeant stationed in Vietnam at the Marine Corp Base in Da Nang as a squad leader in the security company outside the perimeter. I heard his name mentioned and looked him up. I invited him to the slop chute for a cold one. He picked a Seven Up.

"No beer, Sarge?"

"Nope. Just Seven Up."

A few weeks later, the base was bombarded by a heavy mortar attack. Two Marines were killed. Sarge was one of them.

Then one day I started talking to one of his good friends. I mentioned the sergeant, his father-son talks, and all those other strange acts at boot camp.

"Let me tell you about him," he said. "Sometime around 1952, he was a corporal stationed at Camp Lejeune. He had a wife and a two-year-old son. A couple days after Christmas, the wife and kid set out to drive to Maryland to spend a few days with her family. As soon as they left, he high-tailed it to his favorite watering hole to meet his buddies. They had a few beers and got started at the pool table.

"About 2200, the wife and kid were killed in an automobile crash outside of D.C. A drunk driver ran a red light and plowed into the car. They said he was going over sixty miles per hour. The family and the Corps tried for hours to reach the corporal. The chaplain, his platoon leader, and a couple of his friends waited on the front porch. He didn't get home until about 0200, pretty well loaded. Now, Jackson," the sergeant asked me. "Wouldn't you act a little strange?"

Appendix 2

Letters from Bryan

The letters in this appendix were sent to me by Mary Post. Mary's son, Bryan, joined the Corps in 1999 and went through boot camp at San Diego. Mary and Bryan gave me permission to include these letters in this book. Bryan's letters are in chronological sequence. As you read them, notice the transformation of Bryan's feelings, attitude, and disposition.

Bryan did very well in boot camp. He received orders to electronics school, an indication that he is an above-average Marine.

~~~

July 17, 1999

Dear Mom,

I have arrived at MCRD San Diego and am doing well. I am in a training company. My new address is:

Rec Post, Bryan D
2nd Bn "H" Co, Plt 2084
37003 Midway Ave Unit
San Diego, CA 92140-5554

I eat three square meals a day and all my personal needs have been taken care of. Please do not send any large packages because I do not have a lot of room. I will be able to write again very shortly. I will also send info concerning my training. At times I will be asking for info so please respond ASAP. This will help with an easy transition.

A Few Good Memories

~~~

July 23, 1999

Hello Everyone,

Things are going as good as they can, I guess. My platoon is a bunch of undisciplined people, so we are always getting into trouble. They put me on a diet because they say I am over my max weight. So how are things back home? I've been thinking about it a lot. Well I am out of time.

Please make my plane ticket purchase with yours and send me an itinerary. That way we can all sit together. But please make mine to and from the Pasco Airport.

Love,
Bryan

[Note from Bryan's mom:]
Bryan wrote to one of his friends that he hated being on the diet because it reminded him of his days as a varsity wrestler in high school. His wrestling coach was a former Marine drill instructor.

Later, when Bryan was home, he said that the DIs were as tough as his wrestling coach. His former coach also invited Bryan to attend some of the wrestling team's training sessions while he was home on leave.

~~~

July 23, 1999

Dear Mom and Dad,

Hello, me again. Will you please make my plane reservation when you make your own? This would ensure that we get to ride home together. But when you make mine please make them from San Diego to Pasco and from Pasco to San Diego. You should be getting some info in the mail about plane tickets and graduation week. When you make my reservation, please go through the travel company in the brochure.

After graduation, we are not permitted to leave till 1:00 pm. I hope I can make it that long. We are getting in a lot more trouble than we should. I am starting to have free time every night so I can write you. Will you please send me the address book?

So how are things back home? I hope fine. Well, I will talk to you later. Oh yeah—please don't send me any food. Someone received food today and was harassed forever.

Love you all.

Love,
Bryan

~~~

July 26, 1999

Me again. Things are starting to get better here. People are finally getting it together. Thank you for the letter. The training I was talking about was the actual beginning to Boot Camp. We run every day and work out along with drill. We drill the most however.

So how is the computer now? I know you should not have let the kids touch it. Oh well. Have you seen Rachael lately? I have not heard from her. Hope you and the kids had fun camping in the motor home.

Today there was somebody was put on report for not training, or I should say refusing to train.

Well, like I asked you before, could you please buy my plane tickets with yours through the info you get through the mail? Then could you send me an itinerary? Thank you.

So how is Dad doing in my truck? I hope he has not had many problems. But man, the sun down here is just unreal. It is so hot. How about up there?

Could you tell me what all new is going on cuz I'm completely shut off from the outside world. Guess what? You will *never believe it. I'm going to church every Sunday. A Lutheran church at that. So how are you holding up at home? Hopefully pretty good.*

Well, got to get going. I love you.

*Love,
Bryan*

~~~

August 2, 1999

Hello Mom and Dad,

Things are going pretty good for me. I got both the letters you sent me. So, are you going to make my plane reservation with yours? If so, please let me know and send me a copy of the itinerary.

Guess what. I'm off my diet now. I lost all the weight I needed to. Today we did an obstacle course and I did good on it. We have been learning some hand-to-hand combat.

Guess what. I now have a checking account/ATM/debit card. Scary huh? I miss you all back home. Would you please send me updated pictures? Thank you. I just got a letter from Grandma today. Well, love you all. Tell Brianna that I will be home later. I miss you all.

*Love,
Bryan*

~~~

August 9, 1999

Dear Mom,

How are things? Things are all right here. On Saturday we have a drill evaluation. I will let you know how we do. Could you send me wallet-size family pics and a pic of Jacob (the new one)? Thank you.

The other day we did a mock PFT (physical fitness test) and I did 10 pull-ups and 106 crunches and three miles in 21:50 (21 minutes and 50 seconds). So all I need is a few more pull-ups, which I have done before.

I miss everybody back home. I will be home in a couple of months now.

Right now in my checking account I have $184.74. I just got a statement the other day. Also I ordered pics of me in dress blues. So when you come don't buy any. I have plenty. I ordered lots of things like a yearbook.

I'm getting an AT&T military phone card. It will be sent to you so please don't lose it.

The drill instructors have started to act a whole lot harder on us. Just yesterday we went to the pit twice. (We did stuff like push ups, etc.)

Well I got to go. Miss you all. Love you all.

Love,
Bryan

    P.S. How are the fish doing?

~~~

August 9, 1999

Dear Mom,

Could you send me Aunt Donna's full address because you left out the P.O. box number? Thank you. So how are things back home? Is Bree still saying "Bryan?" If she is, tell her that I will be back after something. That way she has an idea. Also could you send me our family pic and pics of the kids and any new ones? I hang them up in my footlocker.

A Few Good Memories

We just had Eval Drill and we failed it. I'm doing good here for now. The DIs lighten up and then get strict. You never know what mood they are going to be in.

Oh yeah, could you send me some envelopes inside the next letter you send so I can continue to write you.

We have learned a lot of drill moves with our M16A2 service rifles. I am actually doing them pretty good.

So how is Jennifer doing? [Jennifer is Bryan's sister.] *I haven't heard from her for a long time—actually ever since I got here.*

Guess what? I set up a bond plan. $50 per month for a $100 a long way down the road. I can cancel the bonds at any time I want after MCT. (Marine Combat Training, the next step after graduation from Boot Camp.) It will be about 3 months. They are going to be holding the bonds for me till I get to my first duty station.

Guess what? I have to do all my laundry by hand. It sucks. Could you please tell me how much money I have in my bank account altogether? That way I can plan things for after Boot Camp and after everything gets settled down. You can use as much as you need for plane tickets.

Before taxes each month I make $887.80. The food here is starting to get really old because for breakfast each morning we have the same thing. Lunch and dinner are just about the same.

Guess what? Two months from today I will be going home. On Monday we will be starting training day 18 (T-18). There are 56 T-days before the Crucible. So, we are a third of the way done I assume.

Remember: Don't buy anything they try to sell you when you come here because I have bought a video, pictures, and a yearbook. They are going to try to sell stuff to you when you come.

You know, after Boot Camp I just might start going to church on Sundays. I might.

Well, I got to go. Love you all and miss you all.

Love,
Bryan

A Few Good Memories

~~~

August 11, 1999

Dear Mom,

I got both of your letters and both of Jennifer's letters plus one from Rachael yesterday.

Today we are getting fitted for our service "A" uniforms. It is cool. We are also getting our names on our cammies. I got the pictures from Jenn and have most of them hung up in my footlocker.

I can't remember if I told you but we failed Eval Drill as a platoon. The DIs have really lightened up. The other day we did the confidence course. It was really fun. We also get to do pugil sticks again soon. The pugil sticks are supposed to represent a fight using your rifle and bayonet. It is fun. I don't have to wear the glasses here because they said my eyes are good to go. I hope it is that way on the rifle range.

We have less free time now so I will write as much as I can. Sometimes I stay up at night to write to you. Right now I have to study a bunch for a test we will be having on T-32.

I'm still doing fine. I'm glad you got your computer back. We finally get to shower on our own now but it takes up some of our free time. You'll never believe it but I am getting good at shining boots.

Well, I got to go. Love you and miss you.

Love,
Bryan

~~~

August 14, 1999

Dear Mom,

A Few Good Memories

How are things? Today I ran my first PFT. I did 13 pull-ups, 103 crunches, and three miles in 20:30. Today I will also be going to Camp Pendleton for a week. It for "team week." I will have the same address and everything. I don't know how much free time I will have up there. I will try to write you as much as I can. I will be working on maintenance. The DIs are really going easy on us lately. Well, I got to go. Time's up.

Love,
Bryan

P.S. I got envelopes at the P.X.

~~~

August 14, 1999

Hello again. It's me. I'm up North (Camp Pendleton) now and I will be on maintenance for the next week. I've been told that I will have some free time. Right now it sucks. We are just sitting down and doing nothing. Camp Pendleton is a really big base from what I can see from the bus ride.

The other day I received my service "A," "B," and "C" uniforms and my service all-weather coat and service sweater. My all-weather service coat is really nice. It is like a dress coat like Mom's, but tannish-greyish with a removable liner.

The DIs I have here at Camp Pendleton are all from "hotel" company and are really strict. Oh well, it's just a week. I passed the PFT test today and learned how to make a linen roll.

The reason I asked you to send some envelopes was I didn't know when my next P.X. call was. I have plenty for now. I'm doing just fine here. At times I wish Josh or someone like that was here to talk to. Oh well, I have made a couple new friends up here. We really don't have a lot of time to talk though. The main thing that keeps me going is letters from home. Could you do me a favor and get me Josh's and Taylor's address? Thank you. I would really appreciate it.

A Few Good Memories

The other day at the P.X. I spent $103.00 on stuff I was told to buy. Plus I bought a Bible and a cross while I was there. Imagine that—me turning religious. The Lutheran services weren't that great but I am living with them. I wish they had some services like Faith did. But, oh well, life goes on.

When I come home I'm going to be so dark from being out in the sun for so long. I can't wait to be able to relax in the pool. I should have done it more when I was home.

I'm getting good at spit-shining boots! It's a miracle. I have to polish a set of boots every night. While I'm up North I will only have to shine one pair of boots. My feet are finally adjusting to wearing boots 24-7.

There haven't been any new changes lately beside team week. Well, I love you and miss you. Got to go.

Love,
Bryan

~~~

August 14, 1999

Dear Mom and Dad,

How are things going? I'm doing good. All I will be doing this week is painting a squad bay. Yesterday we were using paint thinner to clean the floor and there was hardly any ventilation. Needless to say, we all got high in the room. The people in charge were just laughing at us. When we were just about done, they gave us a break to clear our heads. For some people it did not work. The people in charge of me are pretty cool. They let us talk and joke around. They answered a bunch of questions about the Fleet. The only part that sucks is getting up at 2:30 a.m. and going to bed at 21:00 (9 p.m.).

So how is my truck doing? How are my fish? Have they all survived? How is Puddles doing? Fine, I hope. Has he changed much without me there?

Love,
Bryan

A Few Good Memories

~~~

August 17, 1999

Dear Mom and Dad,

Me again. Still up North. Yesterday I worked in the mess hall, cleaning the damn bathrooms all day long. It was clean one, then clean the other. It sucked a whole lot.

I talked to a lot of people in my platoon and they are pretty cool. Up North, things are being stolen like crazy because Platoon 2088 is staying in the same squad bay as us, and they are so undisciplined. Yesterday in the chow hall, a lot of people were getting sent back because they are stupid and undisciplined.

Well, got to go. Love you and miss you.

Love,
Bryan

~~~

August 18, 1999

Dear Mom and Dad,

Hello. Me again. Today I'm painting again. It's pretty cool. I get about four hours of free time a day so I have been writing a lot of letters, as you can see.

So how is everyone back home? The whole time I have been up here at Camp Pendleton, I have not got one mail call. It sucks. All I can do is write letters and hope people are answering back. I miss getting the letters from you and everyone else.

When we go back to San Diego we will be there a little over two weeks, then come up North for four weeks. Then I'm a Marine. After the four weeks up here I go back to San Diego a Marine and they call that week, "transition week." It is going to be cool when I come back up here to finish out the training cycle. For one, there will be only a month left, and too, I will get to fire the M16 that I have.

 Tell everyone back home that I miss them and love them. Well, got to go. Love ya.

Love,
Bryan

~~~

August 19, 1999

Hello everyone,

 Me again. Today we served DIs breakfast. It was cool. The DIs had just finished DI school. Then after it was done we went back to painting. It sucks. All I do any more is paint. Oh, well, it's over tomorrow. I get out of here and back on normal hours.
 I have found out so much while I was up here about training later on that it is going to be easy for me.
 I got to go. Love you all.

Love,
Bryan

~~~

August 22, 1999

Dear Mom and Dad,

 Me again. This week we will be starting swim week. It should be fun. Only six more weeks till I'm a Marine and I can come home.
 The other day I got a letter from Aunt Donna. When you next write could you please send some stamps for I am now out of stamps. Thank you for the envelopes you sent me.
 Things have been the same here. The other day I went to Medical to get my wart taken care of and they said I have to wait

till my next duty station, unless it interferes with my training.
So that's my life. What's going on in yours? Sorry you didn't get the job. Well, got to go.

Love,
Bryan

~~~

August 30, 1999

Dear Mom and Dad,

Hello. It's me. I got quite a lot of letters from you this week. Some were really old. Some were from the 9th and 10th of August. I still liked reading them anyways.

So how was the fair with Aunt Donna and Uncle Bill? Interesting, I bet. I wish I could have gone to fair, but oh well. So did you ever find Rachael while you were out there?

Things here at boot camp have been the same. We just finished swim week and it sucked. You had to swim with all your gear on. If you want to take the pool and close it, go ahead. If I want to swim I can always go to the country club or something. So don't worry. Just do what you need to do.

Yesterday we had an inspection in our service "A" uniforms and I passed. This week we have final drill, final PFT, and practical. I should do good on all. I hope I can do the run for the PFT because I have a real bad cold. I am going to go to Medical shortly because it is so bad.

Sorry I could not have written you more this week but I was pretty busy. I will write you as much as possible. Well, I got to go. Love you all.

Love,
Bryan

~~~

A Few Good Memories

August 30, 1999

Dear Mom and Dad,

I tried to call you today, but nobody was home. They let us make a phone call for travel plans. There is only one piece of info I need. You are going to give me a ride to the airport: right or wrong? Could you let me know ASAP? It is important. Thank you. I have gotten a few letters from you this past week and I enjoy reading them.

Swim week sucks because all you do is swim with all your gear on. Other than that, everything is the same next week. We have final drill practice and something else I can't even remember. Then after that we go up North for four weeks.

Well, I got to go. Times up. Love you. Miss you.

Bryan

~~~

September 2, 1999

Hello again,

Well, I couldn't sleep so I thought I would write. We had Final Drill and guess what? We passed. We also had Practicals and I passeded. Practicals is a 50-questions written test and a 10-question oral test. It was so easy. Some people still failed though; it was weird.

On Saturday we have the final PFT and then we are done with finals week. Well it is time for me to go. Love you all.

Bryan

~~~

Sept 2, 1999

Dear Mom and Dad and Jenn,

A Few Good Memories

Hello again, it's me. I received a letter from you the other day. I'm glad that you enjoyed the fair. Wish I could have been there with you. I know that when I get back, Rachael will be in school. Don't worry. I will spend some time at home.

If you need to shut down the pool, don't let me stop you. I can always somewhere to swim. Swim week sucked because we had to swim with all our gear on. That included our M16s. I only classified as a Class 3 swimmer. I could not go any higher.

I only have five and a half more weeks. I can't wait until you come up here. That's not long.

I got to go. Time is up. Love you all. Hope things are fine. The DIs here are starting to play a lot of games with us. Well, love you all.

Bryan

~~~

September 7, 1999

Dear Mom and Dad and Jenn,

Hello, it's me again. We go up North today. I can't wait because it means I am almost done. Just four more weeks of Hell. The four weeks will go as follows:

Week 1: Grass week—Learn how to fire the rifle and adjust the sights.
Week 2: Qualification week—Fire weapons for qualification.
Week 3: Field week—Survival in the field and in the gas chamber.
Week 4: The Crucible

Then we come back down South and have transition week. We will be Marines and I get to see you guys. I can't wait to go home. I have my plane ticket and bus ticket that I needed. The bus ticket gets me to Camp Pendleton for MCT. It is only a $15 ticket

that will get refunded.
   I'm doing good, but I got to go.

Love,
Bryan

~~~

September 13, 1999

Dear Mom and Dad,

   I'm up at Camp Pendleton again. I have the same address up here so don't worry about that. I won't be able to write as much while I'm up here because we really are busy. Next week we start to qualify with our rifles. We have to shoot in four different positions and from 200, 300, and 500 yards. You have to qualify to graduate. It should be no problem for me. I have been doing good. We have fired our rifles once already. It was cool. Everything up here moves at a really fast pace.
   Right now you wouldn't believe it—I'm down to 158 pounds. The other day we did a beach run. It was cool seeing the ocean again. We don't even leave the base to go on a beach run because it is on the base.
   Well, got to go. Love you all.

Love,
Bryan

~~~

September 17, 1999

Dear Mom and Dad,

   Me again. I'm doing fine. My cold is slowly getting better. I buy cough drops to help me with my cold. Right now we are shooting the M16A2. We qualify tomorrow. It is pretty cool. I can hit a target from 500 yards. Amazing, huh?

I got another letter from Aunt Donna yesterday. It was just one of those, "Hi" and "Bye" letters, but it was nice to hear from her.

Oh! You'll never believe it. The MREs are better than the regular food. Scary, huh?

Well, I miss you and got to go for I am out of time. I'll write you later.

Love,
Bryan

~~~

September 20, 1999

Dear Mom and Dad,

Hey, how's it going? Back home. Only 19 days left. Next week, I start "field week." One night I will be living in the field in just a sleeping bag. The next night I will have a tent with no floor to the tent. We will be doing a lot of field firing and night firing. Plus we will do the gas chamber. Plus we have a beach run. The beach here is pretty cool. We have run on it once and hiked on it once already. When we go down there it makes me forget where I'm at. Brings back memories from when I was younger and we went to the beach and camped.

Well, that's all I have planned for next week. Sorry to hear about your mouth. Well, got to go.

Bryan
[Note: This was the first time Bryan referred to MCRD San Diego as "home."]

~~~

September 27, 1999

A Few Good Memories

Dear Mom and Dad,

Hello. Me again. Only two weeks till I will be home. One and a half till you are here and I get to see you. I'm going to enjoy seeing you guys again.

Field week is over. The gas chamber was nothing big. But now I know why tear gas is called "tear" gas. I would have done great if my eyes could take the stinging. We did a lot of hiking during field week. It was cool. Sleeping under the stars was so neat. I did not get much sleep that night because I was so busy staring at the stars.

If there is any money left in my bank account, you can use it to fix my truck (if needed).

It's Thursday morning at 2:00 a.m. Well I got to go.

Love,
Bryan

P.S. Please bring my watch and belt when you come.

Appendix 3

A New Look at Creationism

November 10th has long been celebrated as the birthday of the United States Marine Corps. Contradictory evidence has recently surfaced, which casts some doubt as to the considered Tun Tavern origin. The following is a secret communiqué smuggled out of Libya by a 102-year old retired Marine officer who was searching for the original Mammaluke sword used by Prestley O'Bannon, and thought to have been buried in the sand dunes near Tripoli by O'Bannon himself.

Fellow Marines. Rumors have surfaced recently that could cast doubt on the aforethought origin and history of the United States Marine Corps. Four years ago, it has just been announced, a group of inquisitive scientists followed a hunch that the discovery of the Dead Sea Scrolls in 1947 did not uncover everything. The group launched a new search. They arrived at the site of the discovery, 15 miles east of Jerusalem, and started digging, scratching, and shoveling dirt. The search continued for years.

Six months ago, a shriveled and barely readable parchment surfaced. Workers carefully packed it into a padded container and called Federal Express. At 0530 the next morning, the package was picked up and delivered to an excited and impatient group in Sweden.

The Helsinki Seven, as they have since been named, headed by Monsieur Franco de Lancelot, transferred the manuscript and its final translation to a British Royal Marine "watering hole" called the Bo Peep, which is located just outside of London. Mr. Jim Ellard, pub manager, assumed control and forwarded the official document, including unlimited publishing rights, to

A Few Good Memories

Georgia, and to the writer of a new book-in-progress. Below is the document translation in full:

"In the beginning was the word, and the word was from the Divine Authority, and all else was darkness and void and without form. So the Divine Authority created the heaven and the earth, the sun, the moon, and the stars, so that the light might pierce the darkness.

"The Divine Authority divided the earth between the land and sea, and these He filled with many creatures.

"The dark, salty, slimy creatures were instructed to inhabit the murky depths of the ocean. The Divine Authority called these greasy characters *sailors.* He dressed them accordingly and bestowed upon them trousers with upside-down legs.

"The flighty creatures of the air He called *airmen.* These He clothed in uniforms that were ruffled and fowl-like and capsuled in Irish pennants. Their uniforms often doubled as pajamas, especially when an airman was laid out in the gutters of some dark street, trying to reach an acceptable level of sobriety.

"The lower creatures of the land the Divine Authority called *soldiers.* With a twinkle in His eye and a sense of humor, the Divine Authority gave these soldiers trousers that were too short, jackets too large, and pockets large enough to cram a pair of hands into, even when holding a peanut butter and jelly sandwich. And to adorn their soldier suits, the Divine Authority created cords and meaningless ribbons, patches, stars, and bells. He gave them emblems and crests and all sorts of shiny things that glittered and devices that dangled and made jingly sounds. When you're the Divine Authority, you have the right to get carried away. Who would dare stop you?

"And on the seventh day at about 2215 hours, the Divine Authority thought about taking a break and lighting the smoking lamp. His work should have been over. But somehow He knew all was not complete. The Divine Authority continued to look down from His command post, down upon the earth, desperately trying to spot His error. Something was missing. Terror reigned in the CP, because when the Divine Authority is displeased, all Hell breaks loose.

A Few Good Memories

"The Divine Authority drew upon the total of His infinite sapience and boundless wisdom, and suddenly the answer came. Yes. The answer came. "Eureka, I have found it!" He said, but had better sense than to run through the streets in his nightgown.

"The Divine Authority, struggling with his idea and exerting a huge effort, created a most divine creature. He called His masterpiece a United States Marine. The Marine was molded in the Divine Authority's own image, and was ordered to protect land, sea and air and let no enemy encroach upon the shores.

"The Divine Authority gave these Marines practical, hardy, elegant and stylish uniforms.

"The Divine Authority gave these new and perfect creatures of Divinity practical uniforms so that they might wage wars against the forces of Satan and other evils. He gave them wear-hardy service uniforms for their daily work and training so they might be kept sharp and ready.

"The Divine Authority created special uniforms of evening dress so that Marines would look elegant, sharp, stylish, and handsome as they escorted their ladies on Saturday nights, and would just damn well impress the hell out of everybody.

"And so it was on this eighth day that the Divine Authority looked down upon the earth and saw that the universe below Him was much better.

"But the Divine Authority wasn't happy. Some-thing was still missing. What about Me, He thought. The answer struck Him. In the course of His labors He had forgotten one thing—He had forgotten to create a set of dress blues for Himself. He did not have His own Marine uniform.

"But then the Divine Authority thought about it, pondered over it, and considered it some more. Centuries later He made a decision. He would NOT create His own set of dress blues.

"Not everybody can be a United States Marine," he sighed. The Divine Authority rested."

Appendix 4

A Few Boot Camp Statistics

A recruit's stay at boot camp allows little time to goof off. In fact every minute of every day is scheduled. Very little individual free time keeps recruits' minds on their purpose. Tight scheduling permits an efficient overall boot camp program. Little time is lost.

The following Parris Island boot camp statistics, as of October 1999, will explain the Corps' motto, "A Few Good Men and Women."

20,000 recruits enter boot camp at Parris Island per year.

17,000 recruits become Marines at Parris Island per year.

Almost 3800 male recruits are in training at any one time.

About 600 female recruits are in training at any one time.

The average age of a male recruit is 19 years and 1 month.

The average age of a female recruit is 19 years and 4 months.

Over 98 percent of recruits are high school graduates.

Training time over the 12 weeks includes 64 days / 1549 hours.

A Few Good Memories

Training hours are broken down as follows:		
Hours	Percent of Total	Description
59.0	3.81	Physical fitness
279.5	18.04	Crucible, weapons, water
41.5	2.68	Core values
54.5	3.52	Close-order drill
31.0	2.0	Field training
27.0	1.74	Close-combat training
13.0	.18	Conditioning marches
60.0	3.87	Administrative
55.5	3.58	SDI time
60.0	3.87	Movement
479.0	30.92	Sleep
210.0	13.56	Basic daily routine
179.0	11.56	Chow

Appendix 5

The Recruit

How many reasons are there for a young person to decide to be a Marine? At first, we might think that love of country would register at the top of the list, but it doesn't always work that way. It seems that for every recruit there is a different and very special reason.

The very helpful and accommodating staff at Parris Island arranged for me to meet and interview ten recruits (five females and five males) who were about eight weeks deep (over half-way) into their training. Major Alday turned his office over to me for "as long as you need it." It was one of the most pleasant and satisfying afternoons I had experienced in years. The gung-ho, soon-to-be warriors, down to the last recruit, had zero regrets. Quality recruits are arriving at boot camp, thanks to the Marine recruiters like SSgt Mike Gross.

Vivian was a young female from Jacksonville, Florida. She had been so impressed by the television program, "JAG," and the character of Marine LtCol Sara McKenzie, played by the stunning Catherine Bell, that she made the decision to join up and try to find a way to be part of the Navy's Judge Advocate General Corps.

Mike Glowacki from Dedham, Massachusetts, entered my office, looking very much like the next Marine Corps Poster Marine. He said that he had had a head start when he served in another branch of the military. But he wanted more spirit, more essence, more pizzazz from the military. At the end of his Army enlistment, he rushed to the nearest Marine recruiter and signed up. Mike ended boot camp as top honor graduate of his platoon, with the meritorious rank of Lance Corporal, and a set of dress blues, compliments of the Corps.

A Few Good Memories
_____

Heather, from Quitman, Georgia, joined the Corps with her boyfriend. They were at Parris Island at the same time. She had gotten a glimpse of him two times, once while both their platoons were on the grinder (drill field), and the second time when both their platoons were training at the 50-feet high rappel tower. She is hoping they'll end up at Camp Lejeune together.

[Note: The Marine Corps is the only remaining branch of the military with separate training for males and females. Our thanks go out to the 55 Marine Generals who threatened resignation a few years ago when President Clinton's Department of Defense pressured the Corps to switch to co-ed training. We're proud of you, Sirs. Let's hope your message was strong enough to withstand future onslaughts. When will politicians keep their noses out of things they really don't understand? Remember, civil servants, don't fix what ain't broke.]

Donald, a recruit from Ohio joined the Corps because he craves activity. "I could never sit at a desk. I want to be a part of the toughest thing around and that's the Marines," he told me. "When I get outta here, I don't want to hold back anything."

Jacqueline from Hollywood, Florida, signed up for the challenge. "I've never really been put to the test," she said. Joining the Corps started with a dare from her friends. She was happy with her decision. She stated that so far, she has never had such challenges in her entire life.

Michael from Rochester, New York, signed up to go to Parris Island to get into armor or "anything that looks like a tank," he said.

The state of Vermont sent Nadia to the Corps. Nadia joined up because her father was a military man, the US Navy. She had considered joining the Navy but felt that being a Marine would go her father one better.

Frankie from Maryland wants aviation mechanics. He said that his entry scores and his aptitude tests were sufficient for the Corps to assure him of his choice.

Silvia, a female recruit of Hispanic descent, is from Richmond Hill, New York. Silvia joined the Marines in appreciation for the opportunity that the United States has given to her family. She joined to "give something back."

Philadelphia was the birthplace of this nation and of Adam. Adam is proud that he shares his name with his father and his grandfather. Having been assured of his MOS choice in aviation electronics, he will be assigned to electronics school after boot camp.

Georgia's most famous Marine tells the story of his decision to join the Corps in his book, *Corps Values*, Longstreet Press, 1996. When Zell Miller was 21 years old, his favorite activity on weekends consisted of carousing and drinking too much North Georgia rotgut moonshine whisky. One Saturday night in August of 1953, the future governor, and later senator, of the state of Georgia, Zell Miller, once again having sopped up a bit too much of the mountain joy juice, sideswiped an automobile and ended up behind bars in Ellijay, Georgia.

A night of reflecting brought this superior man to his senses. During the night, Miller remembered a Marine Corps recruiting poster he had seen in Atlanta: *"The Marines: We Make Men."* He knew this message was directed at him. He high-tailed it down to the nearest Marine Corps recruiting office and signed up for a three-year hitch. Mr. Miller finished Parris Island and matured into the man who would become governor of Georgia and lead the state into becoming one of the nation's most progressive states and subsequently into the position of United States Senator from Georgia.

Brigadier General James Battaglini, former commanding general of the Parris Island Recruit Training Depot, told me that he and Governor Miller once shared lunch on the porch of the General's home at Parris Island. During their meeting, Governor Miller frequently reflected as to what might have been, had he not put his life into the hands of Marine Corps drill instructors.

All Marines, former, present, and future, should read Zell Miller's book. The world should read *Corps Values*. Mr. Miller's 12 essays form an excellent guide to the way *every* life should be lived. I have thus far purchased 14 copies of Senator Miller's book to give to new Marine enlistees from this area. It makes good reading in preparation for boot camp and for life.

Mike D. contributed this story about his decision to join the Marines:

I joined the Corps in 1950 after high school. I had no choice about going into the service. The draft, you know. It was just "which branch?" Most of my friends waited to get drafted because it meant only 18-24 months. But I talked my friend Harry R. into a covenant that we would join the Marines when we graduated.

Harry was tough and I wanted to be. I was sure if Harry went with me, I'd find the courage to last it out.

The last couple of months of our senior year in high school were spent convincing all the girls that they didn't want to go out with some wimpy army draftee. It really worked. We bought some Marine Corps stuff to wear around school. Harry had a junky old convertible and we attached a Marine Corps flag to the radio antenna. The radio didn't work very well, but the flag did. We were already national heroes and we hadn't spent the first night in a barracks.

In April, a month before graduation, I went to nearby Augusta, Georgia, to see the Marine recruiter. He told me I was doing the right thing and gave me a few tests. Afterwards, he told me I passed and asked me some questions about my family. I can still hear the clickety-clack of the manual typewriter sitting atop the gray metal stand.

Those were the days of the quick-enlistment. Recruiters handled everything. He asked me to raise my right hand and repeat after him. The only part of the oath of enlistment that I remember now is that I agreed to defend this country against all enemies. He gave me two Marine Corps bumper stickers and told me that I'd hear from them soon.

A Few Good Memories

The next day I showed Harry the bumper sticker and told him that I was in. All I had to do was pass my physical and then I was off to Parris Island. Now it was up to him. If he hurried, we'd go to boot camp together.

I got the shock of my life when Harry said that his folks wouldn't let him join the Marines. He said that his mama said the Marines were too tough and he should get into something easier. To this day, I'm not really sure whether it was Harry's mama that kept him out of the Corps or whether he, himself, chickened out.

I do know that on that last day in May 1950, when the bus passed through the Parris Island Gate and sped down that mile-long causeway, I was the loneliest and most frightened kid in the country. I was soon to find out that my fears were well founded. I was one of the unfortunate kids to leave the comforts of home to the demands of Marine Corps boot camp, and then into the horrendous Chinese Communist trap at Chosin Reservoir in Korea.

But I would realize years later that the training I received at "The Island God Forgot" and the demands of battle were the most important events of my life. The Corps instilled a personal discipline within me that would help me start Dowell Home Builders and make it a success.

I didn't pressure my son to join the Corps, but in 1980, a few months before his high school graduation, he came to me and said that he had spoken to a Marine recruiter at school. I winced inside, but with pride. Two months after graduation he left for Parris Island. I was proud, but I also felt the fear that I had felt 30 years earlier.

He did well. He earned his PFC stripe out of boot camp. A year later he was promoted to corporal. At the end of his enlistment, he received an honorable discharge, and now is the owner of Dowell Home Builders. He runs it well. I am content to fish and watch Korean War and other Marine Corps documentaries on PBS, and remember, and hope that I am the only person in my family to ever have to face death on the battlefield. But I know that if Michael, Jr., does have to, he'll be ready.

Semper Fidelis

ISBN 155369144-X